The Bahamas

The Bahamas

BY MARTIN &
STEPHEN HINTZ

Enchantment of the World
Second Series

Children's Press®

A Division of Grolier Publishing

NEW YORK   LONDON   HONG KONG   SYDNEY
DANBURY, CONNECTICUT

To the Lucayans, who were here first

Consultant: Janet Henshall Momsen, Ph.D., Department of Human and Community
Development, University of California, Davis

Please note: All statistics are as up-to-date as possible at the time of publication.

Library of Congress Cataloging-in-Publication Data

Hintz, Martin.
      The Bahamas / Martin and Stephen Hintz.
      p. cm. —(Enchantment of the world. Second series)
      Includes bibliographical references and index.
Summary: Describes the geography, plants, animals, history, economy, language,
      religions, culture, sports, arts, and people of the Bahamas.
      ISBN 0-516-20583-8
      1. Bahamas—Juvenile literature. [1. Bahamas.] I. Hintz, Stephen V.
      II. Title. III. Series
      F1651.2.H66 1997
      972.96–dc21   97-596
                                                        CIP
                                                        AC

Acknowledgments

The authors wish to thank all the Bahamian government personnel and tourism officials who took the time to offer suggestions, leads, tips, and contacts for this book. We could not have done it without their good humor, knowledge, patience, and aid. Special thanks go to the individual Bahamians whom we met during our visits to the islands. Cabbies, fishermen, ministers, kids, waiters and waitresses, chefs, farmers, pool attendants, shopkeepers, craftsworkers, authors, guides, musicians, and all the others who gave of themselves to make our job easier. And particular appreciation is extended to intern Kathleen Daley who assisted with research, writing, and copy review. Her assistance was invaluable. The same goes for Daniel Hintz.

Contents

Lighthouse at Nassau

Hello, Bahamas

The flight attendants smile their good-byes and the waiting Bahamian ground crew smiles hello. Welcome to another world. Welcome to Nassau, the capital of the Bahamas, on New Providence Island. This is the official entry point to the Bahamas and the sweet scent of hibiscus fills the air.

ON THE RIDE INTO TOWN, DON'T BE BASHFUL ABOUT ASKING questions. Your cab driver will give you a quick history lesson on the Bahamas. He swerves around the putt-putting little jitney buses, points out the passing sights, complains about the traffic, and still manages to get you safely to your destination. This is your first taste of typical Bahamian friendliness.

Where will you be staying? In a fancy resort hotel? A beach club? Or on one of the Out Islands? (The Out Islands are the Bahamian islands other than New Providence Island.) The Bahamas offer plenty of choices.

Clusters of international resorts around Nassau and Freeport, the country's two largest cities, offer plenty of excitement—from casinos and shopping to gourmet food and water slides. The casinos in these hotels are a mecca for tourists, who play poker, roulette, and slot machines. Luxurious shops tempt visitors with glittering jewelry and crystal. Restaurants serve everything from huge plates of red snapper stuffed with spinach and red peppers to peanut butter sandwiches and burgers. And you can paddle around in the deep, clear swimming pools with their sparkling waterfalls and slides.

Smaller resorts are less crowded and more personal. Bahamian college students run children's programs in the hotels.

Opposite: **A signpost points to the many islands of the Bahamas.**

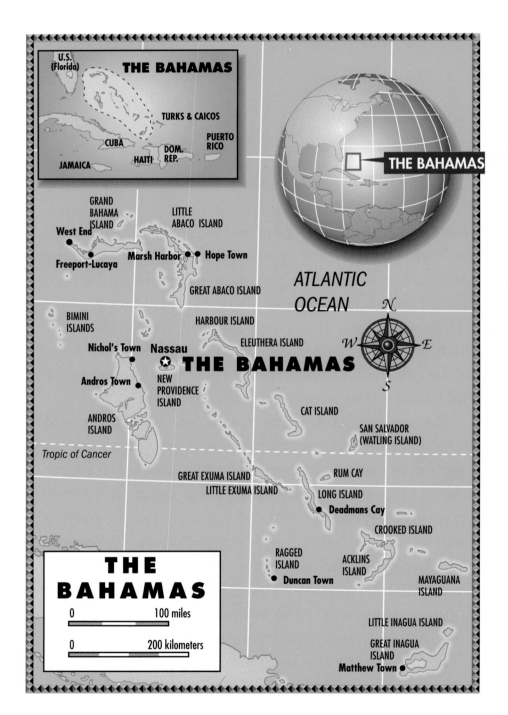

THE BAHAMAS

U.S. (Florida)

TURKS & CAICOS

CUBA

PUERTO RICO

DOM. REP.

HAITI

JAMAICA

THE BAHAMAS

GRAND BAHAMA ISLAND

LITTLE ABACO ISLAND

West End

Marsh Harbor

Hope Town

Freeport-Lucaya

GREAT ABACO ISLAND

ATLANTIC OCEAN

BIMINI ISLANDS

HARBOUR ISLAND

ELEUTHERA ISLAND

N

Nichol's Town

Nassau

W E

Andros Town

THE BAHAMAS

NEW PROVIDENCE ISLAND

S

CAT ISLAND

ANDROS ISLAND

SAN SALVADOR (WATLING ISLAND)

Tropic of Cancer

GREAT EXUMA ISLAND

RUM CAY

LITTLE EXUMA ISLAND

LONG ISLAND

Deadmans Cay

CROOKED ISLAND

RAGGED ISLAND

ACKLINS ISLAND

Duncan Town

MAYAGUANA ISLAND

THE BAHAMAS

0   100 miles

0   200 kilometers

LITTLE INAGUA ISLAND

GREAT INAGUA ISLAND

Matthew Town

Geopolitical map of the Bahamas

They can tell you about life on the Bahamas, teach you to scuba dive, or take you to a local museum or a sports event.

You can enjoy another kind of vacation on one of the Bahamas' more remote islands. Imagine just you and your family in a seaside bungalow. Wide beaches wait for a seashell search, or you can go fishing for grouper, a large reef fish—and watch out for sharks! Explore caves, study the stars, read books. Try waterskiing or parasailing. All these options make the Bahamas a great place to be.

No matter where you stay, you will soon see that the Bahamas are a lot like their neighbors to the north. The people here speak English, though it may be difficult to catch what folks are saying because of their accents and local words. But you can read street signs, menus, and newspapers. Bahamians accept U.S. and Canadian currency as well as Bahamian dollars and cents, so you know how much you're spending on souvenirs. You can see the same television shows, listen to the same music, and talk about the same basketball stars. (But be careful crossing the street:

The Bahamas is a vacation destination for millions of tourists a year.

Bahamian motorists use the left side of the road, just like drivers in Great Britain.)

However, beneath the similarities, the islands are unique. The country has a bold seafaring history, with a bit of pirating thrown in. In spite of their economic hardship over the centuries, the people keep a positive outlook. Bahamians are proud of what they have achieved and look forward to the future.

A String of Islands

The Bahamas are a chain of 700 islands in the North Atlantic Ocean. This chain of islands is called an archipelago. Scattered near the larger islands are more than 2,000 rocky islets and cays (pronounced KEES). The word *cay* was taken from the Indian word *cairi*, meaning "island."

13

THE CLOSEST U.S. CITY IS PALM BEACH, FLORIDA, WHICH IS approximately 50 miles (80 km) to the west. Cuba lies 60 miles (97 km) to the south.

Land Area

The total land area of the Bahamas is 5,382 square miles (13,939 sq km), with more than 2,000 islands spread over 103,000 square miles (266,770 sq km) of blue water. Some 274,000 Bahamians live on twenty-three islands, with more than half in Nassau, on New Providence Island. Some of the islands are uninhabited.

An aerial view of the Exumas—just some of the thousands of Bahamian islands

Most of the islands are low and flat, with wide sandy beaches. Some beaches are dotted with intricate shells and pieces of driftwood, while others are as smooth and clean as your living room carpet. Mount Alvernia, the highest point in the Bahamas, rears its forested crown 206 feet (63 m) above lush Cat Island. High on Mount Alvernia is the tomb of a monk named Father Jerome, who built several churches around the country.

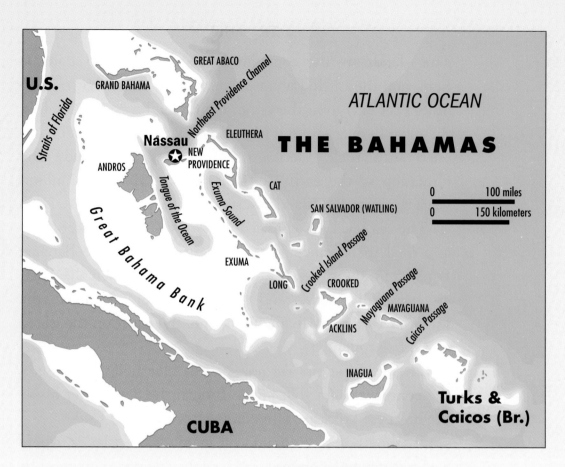

Geographical Features

Largest Island: Andros, 2,300 square miles (5,957 sq km)

Smallest Island: Long Cay, 9 square miles (23 sq km)

Most-Populated City: Nassau (pop. 171,540)

Least-Populated Major Island: Rum Cay (pop. 53) and Ragged Island (pop. 89)

Highest Elevation: Mount Alvernia, 206 feet (63 m)

Lowest Elevation: Sea level

Rivers: None (Most freshwater is imported.)

Terrain: Low and flat

Climate: Semitropical

Average Rainfall in Rainy Season *(May through November)***:** 44 inches (112 cm)

Average Rainfall in Dry Season *(December through April)***:** 2 inches (5 cm)

Average Summer Temperature: 80°F (27°C)

Average Winter Temperature: 70°F (21°C)

Bahama Reefs: 5 percent of the earth's reef mass

World's Largest Flock of Flamingos: 60,000 West Indian flamingos on Great Inagua Island

Blue Holes

The islands are the coral limestone tips of Great Bahama Bank and the Little Bahama Bank, rocky ridges that rise 1.5 miles (2.4 km) from the ocean floor. Coral was deposited on these banks over millions of years. As it dried, the coral hardened into rock. Geologists—scientists who study the formation of the earth—estimate that it took 104 million years to create the islands we see today.

The sea level has changed many times over the centuries and used to be much lower than it is today. The Bahama Banks were then vast, dry, limestone tables. When the glaciers eventually melted and the ocean level rose again, the water covered the Bahama Banks and the caves on the island of Andros collapsed.

The resulting pits are now called "blue holes" because of the eerie blue light that filters through the deep water inside them. These holes are often circular, with straight sides.

"Boiling holes" are found off many of the islands, where freshwater bubbles up from the seafloor. Clearly, there must be some open connection between the islands and the ocean that allows freshwater to escape from the land.

Coral reefs are found on the northern rim of most Bahamas islands. These reefs are made from the skeletons of billions of tiny sea creatures called coral polyps. Over the centuries, the dead polyps pile up to form reefs. Living polyps have brilliant green, orange, red, and other vibrant colors. They are found in warm ocean waters where the currents bring them food. Polyps need sunlight, so they grow only in shallow water.

A thin coating of topsoil and humus covers the islands' rock base. Humus is similar to garden compost—decaying plant matter that helps make soil fertile. Most land in the Bahamas has only a few inches of soil.

Swamps, lakes, and ponds dot the surface of many islands, but there are no permanent rivers or streams here. The rainwater seeps through cracks in the rock to large underground reservoirs. This freshwater usually forms a bubble on top of a saltwater pool. A layer of brackish, somewhat salty water lies between the salt water and the freshwater. The brackish water is drinkable, but it leaves a salty aftertaste. On islands such as Andros where there is more rainfall, the bubble of freshwater

An underwater view of colorful coral polyps

may be more than 100 feet (30 m) deep. On islands like Eleuthera and Little Exuma, the bubbles of freshwater are only a few feet deep.

The Isles of June

The Bahamas are often called "the Isles of June," thanks to their balmy weather. Even in the rainy season, it seems like summer. The sun shines at least seven hours a day. The average summer temperature is 80°F (27°C) and the average winter temperature is 70°F (21°C). Temperatures rarely drop below 60°F (15°C) or rise above 90°F (32°C). Very little rain falls in the dry season. But the wet months (May through November) get up to 44 inches (112 cm), usually in the early morning and midafternoon.

But nothing is perfect, not even here. Hurricanes—fierce tropical storms—may occur between August and November. With winds up to 150 miles (240 km) per hour, they do a lot of damage.

Hurricanes in the Bahamas

When a hurricane is threatening, everyone flees inland. They try to get as high as possible, far from the towering waves that pour over seawalls and docks. Often the raging waters pick up large ships and dump them in the interior of an island. The violent winds peel off roofs, crush buildings, rip down power lines, and generally cause great devastation.

On September 13, 1996, Hurricane Hortense struck the Bahamas. The National Hurricane Center listed Hortense as

The climate on the islands is almost always warm.

The Legendary "Great Bahamas Hurricane"

One of the worst hurricanes in history struck the Bahamas on September 30, 1866. Following the howling wind, a wall of water 60 feet (18 m) high surged out of the ocean and smacked the islands with such force that all the houses on the Out Islands were destroyed. Reports said that the water was as high as the dome of a lighthouse. Entire forests were washed away and crops were buried under mountains of mud. Of the 200 ships moored in Nassau harbor, only one survived intact. Other severe hurricanes have swept across the Bahamas since then (left), but few struck with such fury as the legendary "Great Bahamas Hurricane."

a Category Four—"very dangerous." Maximum sustained winds of 140 miles (225 km) per hour doused the southern islands before moving on in strength over the Atlantic Ocean. Heavy surf from the storm hit U.S. shores shortly afterward. Grand Turk Island was the most heavily hit part of the Bahamas, but no deaths were reported. Hurricane force winds extended 70 miles (112 km) from the eye of the storm.

The generally pleasant climate owes a lot to the Gulf Stream. This warm ocean current flows around the tip of Florida and continues up the eastern coast of the United States and across to Ireland. The current curls around the Bahamas, its warm blue waters contrasting with the cold gray-green of the North Atlantic Ocean. The Gulf Stream travels as far north as Canada and then turns east to flow across the Atlantic. There, it warms the west coast of Europe, generally keeping that continent's harbors ice-free in the winter.

Now that you've been introduced to the islands, let's take a closer look at some of them.

The Abacos

The Abacos are a chain of islands stretching from Walker's Cay in the north to Hole-in-the-Wall in the south, and covering an area of 650 square miles (1,684 sq km). Approximately 10,000 people live in the quiet villages of the Abacos. The Bahamians call these "the family islands" because everyone who visits here is considered part of the family. Also, their protected waters and isolated coves make them a fine place for deepwater sailing.

Hope Town, on the east coast of Great Abaco, is a popular layover. The town is noted for its candy-cane-striped lighthouse. The lighthouse is just a short stroll from the harbor, past the tiny post office and the Wyannie Malone Historical Museum with its shipwreck displays. Island residents used to earn a living by salvaging material from wrecked ships.

One hundred circular steps lead to the top of the lighthouse, and most visitors agree that the view of the picturesque

harbor is worth the climb. From the catwalk, you can see the village below, making it one of the most frequently photographed sites in the Bahamas.

Hope Town lies on the east coast of Great Abaco.

Andros

Andros is the largest Bahamian island. Actually, it is a collection of four islands separated by narrow tidal channels. Andros covers an area of 2,300 square miles (5,957 sq km) but has only 8,155 residents. The major towns stand along the northeastern coast while the southern areas are more remote and secluded. The inland lakes, swarming with fish, make Andros a paradise for fishing fans.

Opposite: **The candy-cane-striped lighthouse that overlooks Hope Town is a local landmark.**

A 140-mile (225-km) reef lies along the east side of Andros Island. Scuba divers from all over the world flock here to explore the shallow reef and its surroundings. The clarity of the water makes the vibrant colors visible to the naked eye. Divers need to be careful, however. Close to shore, the seafloor plunges 6,000 feet (1830 m) into an underwater valley called the Tongue of the Ocean.

Bimini

Bimini is a small chain of islands consisting of North Bimini, South Bimini, Cat Cay, and Gun Cay. This 9 square-mile (23-sq-km) area is proud of its title as Big Game Fishing Capital of the World. The Gulf Stream, which sweeps along the western shore, brings marlin, sailfish, bluefin tuna, wahoo, and many other big-game species.

North Bimini is more crowded than the other islands. The streets are so narrow that cars must pull over to let other cars pass, and the houses practically touch. But with a population of only about 1,600, it isn't that hard to escape the hustle and bustle of everyday life. On a clear night, the glow of the city lights of Miami can be seen from North Bimini.

Opposite: **Scuba divers explore part of the underwater valley called Tongue of the Ocean.**

Eleuthera and Harbour Island

Eleuthera, the first Bahamian island to be settled, has a population of some 10,000. In 1649, a band of English families sailed from Bermuda seeking religious freedom. They were shipwrecked on the northern end of Eleuthera and settled there. These Adventurists, as they were called, held services in Preacher's Cave. A large rock was used as a pulpit and holes in the roof of the cave allowed in light, much like a cathedral.

A rougher bunch of characters hung out at Spanish Wells. This rocky islet off the northern tip of Eleuthera was a haven for heavily armed pirates. They set up camps there, seeking

The pink sand beaches of Harbour Island

This bridge connects the islands of Little Exuma and Great Exuma.

freshwater and a safe place to store their stolen treasure. Today, most people in the village make their living by fishing for "lobster," another name for Bahamian crawfish.

Just off Eleuthera is Harbour Island, famous for its pink sand beaches and clear turquoise waters. They make it "the prettiest island" in the Bahamas, according to travel agents.

The Exumas

On to the Exumas, whose 365 cays with all their beaches and harbors are a welcome sight for any sailor. The cays sprawl out over 130 square miles (337 sq km). The two main islands of Great and Little Exuma are connected by a bridge across Ferry Channel. Some cays consist of uninhabited sand dunes and rocks sprinkled with salt ponds, some have cliffs that plunge into the surf, and some are covered with dense pine forests. The total population of the Exumas is about 3,500.

Grand Bahama

Grand Bahama Island covers an area of 530 square miles (1,373 sq km) and is home to some 41,000 people. The island is barely 60 feet (18 m) above sea level.

This island was quiet and peaceful until the 1960s, when real estate developers built sprawling golf courses, tennis courts, trendy hotels, and flashy casinos in the Freeport-Lucaya area. However, the oldest settlement on the Grand Bahama, West End, is still calm and quiet.

Grand Bahama also has the nation's largest deepwater harbor, making it easy for freighters to dock. Cement plants, oil refineries, and other industries sprang up next to the harbor, making it less than ideal as a vacation spot.

Freeport-Lucaya

Located: on Grand Bahama Island

Population: 26,574

Founder: American financier Wallace Groves, in 1955

Major Sites: Freeport Harbour, the world's largest privately owned harbor; Garden of the Groves, a 12-acre (5 ha) Garden of Eden with more than 5,000 varieties of shrubs, trees, and flowers; International Bazaar, a collection of restaurants and shops designed by a famous Hollywood special-effects artist

With about 80 percent of the population, Nassau and Freeport-Lucaya are the major cultural, political, and economic centers of the Bahamas.

The Bahamas has some 200 bird species, including the long-necked, stick-legged flamingos, flying here over Great Inagua.

Inagua

Inagua is made up of Great Inagua and Little Inagua—the hottest and driest of the islands. With wide stretches of sand and salt flats, the area has a desert climate. Half of Great Inagua near Lake Rosa is a protected park, a sanctuary and breeding territory for more than 60,000 West Indian flamingos—the national bird of the Bahamas.

Long Island

Long Island is an appropriate name for this island, which is 80 miles (128 km) long and only 4 miles (6 km) wide. Along the shore, many limestone caves are hidden beneath the sea and several shipwrecks lie in the nearby shallows. The island is noted for its beaches—so white they are almost blinding.

Long Island's tough grass once made sheep-raising a profitable business. Today, a few semi-wild sheep and goats can still be seen wandering about the low hills and dunes. Long Island has a population of about 3,400, most of which live in a pleasant village with the unsettling name of Deadmans Cay.

New Providence

Nassau, the capital of the Bahamas, is located on New Providence Island. About 171,540 people, or 60 percent of the country's population, live in this city. Nassau's nightlife sparkles with upscale restaurants, glitzy bars, pounding dance halls, and casinos ablaze with lights at Cable Beach and on Paradise Island.

Map of the Bahamas' natural resources

The Houses of Parliament and the Supreme Court are located here in the governmental and historical center of the Bahamas. Several forts over the harbor date from the 1700s. The water tower near Fort Fincastle, the highest point on the island, stands 200 feet (61 m) above sea level and provides a grand view of the city.

But if you want a low-down look at the waters around New Providence Island, try the Coral World's undersea laboratory. There you can look stingrays and sharks in the face as they swim around outside the plate glass that surrounds you. You can also mail a postcard there in the world's only undersea mailbox.

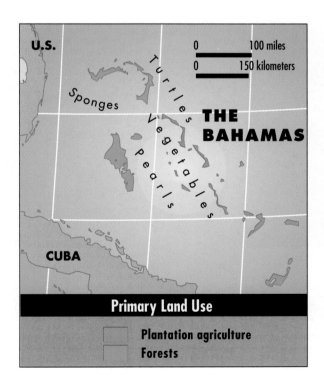

U.S.

0   100 miles
0   150 kilometers

Sponges

Turtles

Vegetables

Pearls

THE
BAHAMAS

CUBA

Primary Land Use

Plantation agriculture
Forests

One of several monuments to Christopher Columbus on San Salvador

San Salvador was originally named *Guanahani* by Lucayan Indians, its first inhabitants. The island was renamed *San Salvador*, meaning "Holy Savior," by Christopher Columbus when he discovered this land in 1492. Four monuments, including a white cross facing the ocean, mark sites where it is believed the explorer first landed. An underwater plaque marks the spot where his ship anchored.

San Salvador (also known as Watling Island) consists of 63 square miles (163 sq km) of sand dunes and rocky ridges, with the 10-mile (16-km) long Great Lake in the center. Many of the island's population of some 465 fishermen and their families live in Cockburn (pronounced KOH-burn) Town, on the west coast. On the east coast, the New World Museum houses many Lucayan relics.

Christopher Columbus was the first tourist to the area. Indeed, he wrote at great length in his journal about the island's beauty. Standing on the top of the Dixon Hill Lighthouse, it is easy to see why.

Flowers, Fins, and Feathers

Bahamians love their colorful flowers. Some grow in the wild and some grow in formal English gardens, a memory of the islands' British heritage. The islands' tropical flowers include hibiscus, bougainvillea, orchid, and oleander.

THANKS TO THE MODERATE CLIMATE, PLANTS IN THE BAHAMAS grow year-round, though fertile soil is scarce. An island's geographical position determines how much plant life it has and what types of plants grow there. However, temperatures are similar throughout the islands.

Vegetation is heavier on the northwestern islands because they receive up to three times as much rain as islands in the south. Extended forests of Caribbean pine are found on Grand Bahama, Abaco, Andros and, to some extent, on New Providence. Grasses, bushes, and lovely orchids grow in the forests where the sun peeks through the treetops. On Paradise Island, leafy casuarina trees form arches over the roads.

Island Trees

The timber business is an important industry on the islands but much valuable hardwood was chopped down years ago, leaving few remaining stands of ironwood, mahogany, or a tropical tree called the braziletto. The lumber was used for boat-building, furniture, and homes. Today, pine plantations stretch in long, ramrod-straight rows on many of the islands. While this ensures a crop for the long-term future, the variety of the natural forests is gone.

Forest fires have also cut the growth on several islands. A hurricane that hit South Abaco in 1962 killed thousands of pines and many damaged trees were not replaced. An infestation of beetles that followed the storm wiped out even more forestland.

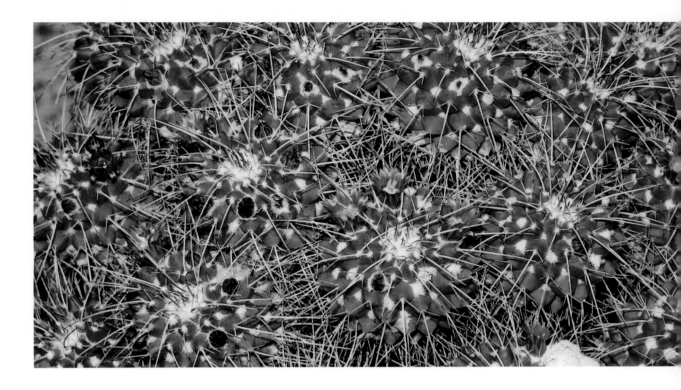

Wooly-nipple cactuses

There are still a few natural forests on the wetter islands of Grand Bahama and Abaco, where evergreen trees reach 30 feet (9 m) high. A hiker needs a machete or sharp knife to chop through the thick undergrowth. On Mayaguana and other dry southern islands, the evergreen trees rarely grow more than 15 feet (4.5 m) high, and there is little undergrowth. It is easier here to walk through the forests. On Inagua, the trees are seldom more than 7 feet (2 m) tall and separated by wide expanses of rock and sand. The wooly-nipple cactus—a 6-inch (15-cm) plant ball of sharp spikes—also grows on Inagua.

Farmers often chop down trees to make room for fields. Sometimes they burn off the plant ground cover, leaving a

Lignum Vitae: The National Tree

Lignum vitae (the "wood of life") is the national tree of the Bahamas. When it blossoms, delicate purple flowers peek out from its lush olive-green leaves. The tree is found mostly in the southern islands. Its common name is *guayacans*. Its very hard, oily wood was once used to make bearings for steamship propellers. Its leaves were used to treat rheumatism and skin disease. Today, lignum vitae is used to make furniture.

nutrient-rich ash that fertilizes their crops. The taller trees are usually left standing for shade. If not constantly cut back or burned off, the brush would crowd out the crops.

Bahamian plant life adapts well to its surrounding climate and the amount of available water. Red mangrove, which looks like a bush, is actually a tree with stiltlike roots that allow it to grow in shallow swamps. The tree is seldom more than 5 feet (1.5 m) tall except near salt ponds, where the red mangrove towers 20 feet (6 m) high. Black mangrove is a taller tree that grows in deeper water.

Towering palm trees and shorter palms called palmettos grow almost everywhere on the islands. The thatch-top palm and the cabbage palmetto are found on low-lying land where there is lots of freshwater. The silver-top palm prefers even wetter conditions, growing well on Andros with its abundant rainfall.

Plant Life

Fragrant frangipani bushes grow wherever their hardy roots find a bit of soil. And some plant varieties grow well in the sand. Sea grape, oat grass, vines, and coco plum bushes are plentiful along the coasts. Their wiry branches and tough leaves stick out of the dunes and their roots help stabilize the shifting sands.

Other Bahamian plants prefer muddy, wet areas. On several islands, thick colonies of one-celled algae spread like

Sea grape trees can be found all along the coasts of the islands.

Tube coral

grape jelly over mud flats near the ocean. According to the weather, they dry out and then are rejuvenated when it rains. Some of the algae clumps look thick enough to walk on, but don't do it. Algae are very fragile and easily injured.

Ocean Life

Numerous types of corals make up the reef with wispy sea fans and straw-colored sea feathers. Tube coral looks like an explosion of small cylinders growing from a central point. Bush coral has many branches and stems that poke into the moving water like a bush on dry land. The long and heavy elkhorn coral gets its name because it looks like the antlers on an elk. Other varieties include green cactus, staghorn, scroll, blushing star, brain, and golfball coral.

To look at the animals of the Bahamas, let's start at the edge of the ocean. More than 650 varieties of shells wash up

Elkhorn coral

Brain coral

along these shores. Within the major shell groups are sub-species—like cousins in families. For instance, there are at least sixteen kinds of Wentletrap shells, each a tiny bit different than the rest depending on where they are found. Collecting seashells is a favorite hobby among young Bahamians. Abaco and the waters of Exuma Sound are great places to look for shells.

A conch emerges to show its stalk eyes.

Divers like looking for conch, a large mollusk with delicious meat inside its heavy white and pink shell. Conch is a basic food for island residents. The meat of the conch is used to make many delicious dishes, from calorie-conscious salads to cornmeal fritters. The empty shells are sold as souvenirs.

Banded coral shrimp, coral crabs, sea urchins, sea cucumbers, the common sea fan, and plume worms are among the more basic life forms found on the seabed and the reefs. Moray eels and dark purple sponges can also be found hiding among the coral.

Undersea life also thrives in manmade "reefs" in the Bahamas. *Theo's Wreck*, a large freighter, was deliberately sunk off Grand Bahama Island in 1982. The wreck rests at the end

A moray eel on the seabed

of the Grand Bahama Ledge, a 2,000-foot (610-m) drop to the main ocean floor. The wreck was named after the Bahama Cement Company manager who came up with the idea of using the old ship to make the fish hotel.

The list of fish species in the islands goes on and on. The warm Bahamian waters are like rush hour on the freeway. Moving with the current are red hind, bluestriped grunt, porkfish, turbot, queen triggerfish, scrawled filefish, spotfin butterfly fish, yellow goatfish, yellowtail snapper, and dozens of others. Some flit by in schools; others prefer to travel alone. The fish range in size from smaller than a finger to the 500-pound (226-kg) jewfish. Some deepwater fish such as jacks, goggle-eyes, and runners return to the reefs to feed.

Swimming with Dolphins

The Underwater Explorers Society offers the Dolphin Experience to let divers interact with dolphins. First, there is a "get acquainted" session in a large bay at the society's headquarters near Freeport. Then divers and dolphins are taken out in the ocean. The dolphins are set free in 50 feet (15 m) of water where they play with the divers.

Also rolling through the water are great sea turtles, whose meat and eggs were considered delicacies by the original inhabitants of the islands. Some turtle species are now protected by law.

Boats heading out to sea often pass giant stingrays flapping along just under the surface of the water. Farther out in the ocean are barracudas, tuna, amberjack, and kingfish.

Not all the fish live in the open sea. Small blind fish who live in permanent darkness can be found in The Cave, at the edge of the ocean on Eleuthera. Centuries ago, their ancestors may have been trapped in underwater pools, where, over time, they slowly adapted to their dark new homes.

Sharks also thrive in Bahamian waters. The famed Shark Hole of Hatchet Bay on Eleuthera is a prime viewing area. A winding road through some scrub brush leads through the old Hatchet Bay Plantation to the cliffs overlooking the ocean. Workers from a nearby poultry-processing plant come down the trail and toss unusable chicken parts into the sea. Immediately, huge sharks fight over the food. Their toothy jaws take the food in great gulps.

Sharks thrive in the warm waters of the Bahamas.

The coloring of stingrays can be quite beautiful.

The Flamingo

The flamingo is the national bird of the Bahamas. It has peach- or rose-colored feathers and a black tip at the end of its beak. A wading bird related to herons and storks, the flamingo has webbed feet like ducks and geese. A flamingo's long legs allow the bird to tiptoe through shallow water and along mud flats to catch small fish.

The famous flamingos of Ardastra Gardens and Zoo on New Providence stand like soldiers on parade when their handlers call them to attention. Responding to handclaps from trainers, they strut along in groups, marching in step. When several claps tell the birds to make an "about-face," they turn in unison and march in the opposite direction.

The Cuban Parrot

Only a few Bahamian parrots remain from the vast flocks that were said to have blocked out the sun when the first European explorers arrived. Actually, this parrot is officially known as *Amazona leucocephala*, or the Cuban parrot. By the 1930s, it existed only in Abaco, Great Inagua, Cuba, and the Cayman Islands. The parrot's green coloring makes it almost invisible in the treetops. It has a white forehead, with rose-colored feathers at its throat and breast, and blue wings. The parrot uses its short round bill to eat fruit and climb up tree trunks.

Protected Areas

Several areas are set aside to ensure that the wild inhabitants of the Bahamas are protected. The rare Cuban parrot, for example, lives in Abaco in a forest supported by the Bahamas National Trust and a group called the Friends of the Abaco Parrot.

In addition to the National Trust lands, another major nature preserve is the Pelican Cay Land and Sea Park at Marsh Harbour in Abaco. And the rare green sea turtle is

Green sea turtles are several feet long and weigh hundreds of pounds.

making a comeback at Union Park on Inagua. These preserves can be enjoyed by hikers on land, while scuba divers can explore the offshore waters.

Island Animals

Many animals brought to the Bahamas either escaped from their owners or were abandoned. Without natural predators to keep them in check, they became pests. Today, wild horses and hogs live in the forests of Abaco, while wild donkeys roam the grasslands of Inagua. Raccoons and rats get into garbage, eat the eggs of nesting birds, and spread disease.

Two animals are native to the islands. A hairy rodent about the size of a rabbit called the utis is one of the few animals mentioned by early explorers that still lives in the

Bahamas. Now protected by law, it lives in brushy areas of New Providence and Grand Bahama.

One of the largest animals on the islands is the iguana—a lizard that grows up to 4 feet (1.2 m) long. It looks scary—like a miniature dragon—but the iguana is a vegetarian and avoids people whenever possible. The iguana is also protected today.

Curly-tailed lizards, frogs, and nonpoisonous snakes also live on the Bahamas. A boa constrictor named Benjamin is a popular resident at the Ardastra Gardens and Zoo. If you are brave enough, a snake handler will wrap Benjamin around your neck to make a living necktie.

A rock iguana

Through History's Looking Glass

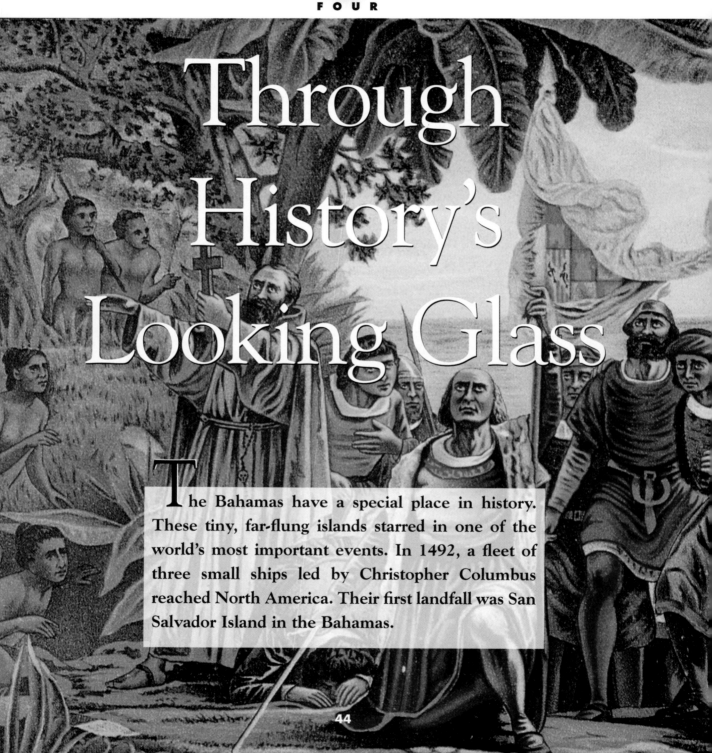

The Bahamas have a special place in history. These tiny, far-flung islands starred in one of the world's most important events. In 1492, a fleet of three small ships led by Christopher Columbus reached North America. Their first landfall was San Salvador Island in the Bahamas.

Christopher Columbus

COLUMBUS'S VOYAGE WAS ONE OF many explorations conducted by Europeans during the Golden Age of Discovery in the 1300s and 1400s. Kings wanted to find passages to the fabled riches of the Orient. Because the overland journey was long and dangerous, sea routes were sought. Europeans wanted the spices of China and India. At first, no one wanted to venture beyond the Canary and Azores islands, the last islands west of the European mainland. Beyond these tiny tips of land were the cold, gray waters of the Atlantic Ocean. No one knew what they might find on the other side.

But Columbus was brave enough to think it would be faster to cross the open sea to the Orient. He convinced the king and queen of Aragon and Castille, two kingdoms on the Spanish peninsula, that his plan would work. The royal couple agreed to fund his exploration.

Columbus Sets Out

The *Santa María*, *Niña*, and *Pinta* left Spain in September 1492, with enough supplies for about 300 days. Despite their initial enthusiasm, the crews became afraid. They were dis-

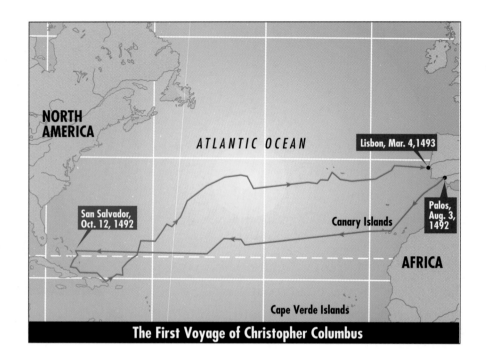

NORTH AMERICA

ATLANTIC OCEAN

Lisbon, Mar. 4, 1493

San Salvador, Oct. 12, 1492

Canary Islands

Palos, Aug. 3, 1492

AFRICA

Cape Verde Islands

The First Voyage of Christopher Columbus

A painting of Columbus landing on San Salvador on October 12, 1492

couraged after the long, dull months at sea. The sailors were totally on their own, as if they had dropped off the face of the earth. And that's exactly what many people in Europe thought would happen. Imagine the crew's relief at 2 A.M. on October 12 when Rodrigo de Triana, a young lookout on the *Pinta*, shouted, *"Tierra! Tierra!"* ("Land! Land!").

When the ships eventually anchored off the coast of San Salvador, the crew thought they might be wrecked on the long reefs and rocky shallows. Looking out at the surf, they called their discovery *gran bajamar*, meaning the "great shallows." Over the years, the pronunciation and spelling changed, becoming "the Bahamas."

Lucayan Indians

Christopher Columbus did not find an uninhabited land when he landed in 1492. The Lucayans, a peaceful group of Arawak Indians, had settled there centuries earlier. Some historians think the Lucayans' ancestors sought refuge from attacks by another Indian group called the Caribs. The term "Caribbean" comes from those long-ago warrior people.

The Lucayans were as surprised to see the Europeans as Columbus was to see them. They fled into the forest when the bearded white sailors landed. Eventually they were lured into the open and brought parrots and cotton cloth to trade for beads.

This depiction of Lucayan life before the arrival of Columbus hangs in the Nassau Museum.

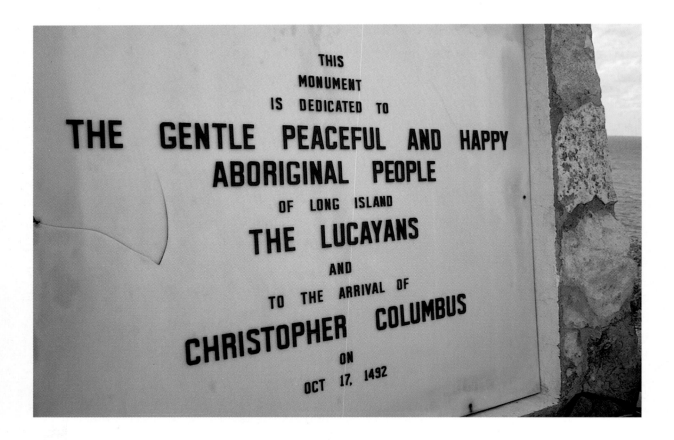

THIS
MONUMENT
IS DEDICATED TO
THE GENTLE PEACEFUL AND HAPPY
ABORIGINAL PEOPLE
OF LONG ISLAND
THE LUCAYANS
AND
TO THE ARRIVAL OF
CHRISTOPHER COLUMBUS
ON
OCT 17, 1492

A plaque on Long Island

Columbus wrote in his journal that these friendly people would make excellent servants. He called them "Indians" because he thought he was near India.

Columbus stayed on San Salvador only a short time. He soon moved on, hoping to find gold and jewels elsewhere. He kidnapped several Lucayans and took them back to Spain. They never returned to their homeland. Columbus made three more voyages to that part of the world over the next several years. He never discovered a passage to the Orient, but his adventures changed the world.

The Lucayans were early victims of this invasion of outsiders. Within twenty years, all of the estimated 40,000 original inhabitants of the Bahamas were dead from overwork and diseases introduced by Europeans. Their culture disappeared when they were made slaves. They were worked to death in the gold mines and on the cotton plantations of islands throughout the region. When all the Indians had died, the white settlers replaced them with slaves brought from Africa. The descendants of these black slaves are now proud citizens of the independent Bahamas.

Ponce de León

One of the next European adventurers who visited the Bahamian islands was Ponce de León. In 1513, the Spanish explorer set out to find the "Fountain of Youth." Anyone drinking water from the legendary freshwater spring was supposed to remain young forever. Among the islands he explored were Inagua, Rum Cay, and Bimini, but he never found what he was seeking.

Ponce de León went to the Bahamas in search of the "Fountain of Youth" in 1513.

Apr. 8, 1513

Jun. 11, 1513

Aug. 6, 1513

ATLANTIC OCEAN

Leaves Puerto Rico March 1513

The Voyage of Ponce de León, 1513

The English were not far behind the Spanish in seeking places to settle and plunder. In 1629, King Charles I of England gave permission for Sir Robert Heath to expand the British colonies in North America. In addition to the Carolinas on the North American mainland, the king tossed in the Bahamas and several other islands for good measure.

The Bahamas were formally taken over by Great Britain on October 30, 1629. A plaque commemorating this event is mounted on the wall of the House of Assembly in Nassau. A portrait of Heath hangs in the city's public library.

A religious war was the real reason why the English settled the Bahamas. A dispute in England arose between the Puritans and the Anglican Church, which was founded by King Henry VIII. Believing that there was no higher religious power than God, the Puritans rejected the king as head of the church. The controversy even affected a far-off English colony on Bermuda, a small cluster of islands about 580 miles (933 km) east of North Carolina.

Sir Robert Heath took over the Bahamas in the name of Great Britain in 1629.

Adventurers and Other Settlers

In 1648, a group of seventy Puritans led by Captain William Sayle left Bermuda. They called themselves the Adventurers. They wanted a country where there was freedom of worship and where everyone would work together.

The Adventurers were shipwrecked off the coast of one of the Bahamian islands. They named it *Eleuthera*, a Greek word meaning "freedom." The Adventurers tried farming on the islands, but the soil was poor. The settlers had to trade wood for provisions sent by other Puritan colonies in the New World. Harvard University in Cambridge, Massachusetts, was built with braziletto timber that came from Eleuthera.

In 1656, another group of Puritans arrived in the Bahamas. They named their island New Providence because of their links with Providence, Rhode Island, and to distinguish the colony from Old Providence off the coast of Nicaragua. All these social and religious experiments failed because the islands were too remote and poor to allow settlers to protect or feed themselves. By 1670, only 1,100 men, women and children remained in the Bahamas.

A Haven for Pirates

This was a bloody time in history. English and French pirates raided Spanish ships carrying gold from South America to Spain. One writer described the pirates as being "thick as wasps around a jampot." Some islanders even lured the ships to the reefs where they were wrecked. The vessels were then looted by the "wrackers."

The capture of the pirate Blackbeard, also known as Edward Teach, in 1718

From 1670 to 1684, the Bahamas were closely linked to the Carolina colonies in America. The Proprietors, a group of wealthy businessmen, were given the right to colonize the Bahamas. Since farming was difficult, residents found they could make a better living from piracy. They regularly attacked Spanish ships. The Spanish eventually fought back. They attacked Charles Town, the original name for Nassau, and destroyed the settlement in 1684.

From the 1600s to the early 1700s, Nassau was a haven for pirates. Calico Jack Rackham, Henry Morgan, William Kidd, and their men were a rough bunch. Anne Bonney and Mary Read were women pirates. They fought and swore more than the men. Edward Teach, known as Blackbeard, made Fort Nassau his headquarters. According to legend, Blackbeard always carried six loaded pistols in his belt. He also tied slow-burning sulfur matches under his hat, framing his face with fire when he went into battle.

By 1718, the British government, sick and tired of pirates, appointed Woodes Rogers as royal governor of the Bahamas. Rogers—a former pirate himself—knew how to deal with the enemy. He attacked and killed them wherever he could. Life as a pirate was not glamorous, and if captured, they were hanged. Their bodies drooped from the gallows where the British Colonial Hotel now stands in Nassau.

Rogers's slogan, "Piracy Expelled, Commerce Restored," remained the Bahamas' national motto until the islands gained independence from Great Britain in 1973. (At that time, Prime Minister Lynden Pindling replaced it with "Forward, Upward, Onward Together.")

Subsequent strong British governors encouraged trade instead of piracy. However, the islands were caught up in the Revolutionary War and its aftermath. In 1776, a fleet of American warships captured the lightly defended Nassau. Hardly a shot was fired and no one was injured on either side. The Americans came back in 1778, threatening to burn the city, but they left after only two days.

British Privateers and Militia

During the war years of 1775 to 1783, the Bahamas became wealthy because British privateers operated out of its ports, raiding American and Spanish shipping. The Spanish, who occupied Nassau in 1782, attacked the Bahamas again.

The Vendue House in Nassau was originally a slave market.

In 1783, the British militia led by Colonel Andrew Deveaux recaptured the city. Deveaux fooled the Spanish into surrendering without much of a fight. After the war, the Bahamas were officially returned to Great Britain.

With the victory of the American colonists in the Revolutionary War, thousands of loyal British citizens fled to Canada and the Bahamas. Between 1783 and 1788, the population of the islands tripled.

The Loyalists left their mark on the islands. Many of Nassau's public buildings were built at that time. The country's first library was established and the first newspaper published.

The End of Slavery

Since many Loyalists were plantation owners from the old colonial South, they brought their slaves with them. This increased the Bahamian slave trade. For years, West African captives from the Mandingo, Hausa, Ibo, and Yoruba tribes were sold in the islands. The Vendue House on Bay Street in Nassau was the islands' main slave market. It now houses the Pompey Museum, named after the leader of a nineteenth-century slave revolt in the Exumas Islands.

Although there were free blacks in the Bahamas, they did not vote until 1807 and only four were members of the Assembly in 1834. That year, the Emancipation Act, which outlawed slavery throughout the British Empire, was passed. (Slavery still existed in the United States.) To ease the transition between slavery and freedom, a system of apprenticeship was established from 1834 to 1838, where former slaves were paid by their former masters.

Blockade Runners and Rumrunners

The American Civil War brought more prosperity to the islands. Southern blockade runners carried cotton to the Bahamas. From the islands, the cotton could be sent on to English mills. On their return, the blockade runners brought medicine and other supplies to the Southern states. These swift ships had to escape a net of Union warships.

During the American Civil War, workers in Nassau unloaded cotton from blockade runners. The cotton was later shipped to English mills.

Nassau's Bay Street boomed with warehouses and docks built to accommodate the blockade runners. When the war ended in 1865, the bottom again dropped out of the island economy.

After the war, the economic slack was taken up with sponge-fishing and farming. Unfortunately, the sponges eventually ran out, and farming was never really profitable. Crops failed or buyers found cheaper products elsewhere.

The business slump that started around the turn of the century lasted for twenty years. One in five Bahamian citizens left the islands to find work. It is estimated that 10,000 to 12,000 Bahamians emigrated and most never returned. Many of them went to Florida to work in the construction and citrus industries.

Large numbers of Bahamian citizens enlisted in the British West Indian and Canadian forces during World War I. They fought bravely on the front lines in Europe. Memorials to these soldiers stand in Parliament Square in Nassau and in settlements around the islands.

In 1919, the United States passed the Volstead Act, which prevented the manufacture and sale of alcohol, and became

Barrels of whiskey and rum sit on the docks of Nassau to be loaded on ships headed for the United States during the Prohibition.

the Eighteenth Amendment to the U.S. Constitution. But Americans still wanted their liquor. "Rumrunners" used the open borders between Canada and the United States. The waters between the United States and the Bahamas were also used to bring in illegal whiskey.

Speeding motorboats sneaked their cargo into Florida. Larger boats took loads as far north as New York. It was like the Civil War blockade days: money

was everywhere. There was even an annual Bootleggers' Ball at the old Lucerne Hotel in Nassau. The Bahamas government earned millions of dollars by collecting customs taxes on every bottle of liquor that came through Nassau.

Sponge-fishing was a profitable business in the Bahamas until the turn of the century. This crew works clipping sponges.

The Great Depression

But the boom did not last. In the late 1920s and 1930s, a worldwide economic slump hit. The Bahamas did not escape this Great Depression. People lost their savings as banks closed and the value of money dropped. In addition, the Eighteenth Amendment was repealed in the United States in 1933, which meant that rumrunners were no longer needed.

Yet during these difficult times, shrewd businessmen like H. G. Christie and Harry Oakes never gave up hope. They bought thousands of acres of land on New Providence to build hotels and golf courses. Oakes, a Canadian millionaire, constructed the first airfield in the Bahamas.

During World War II, the building of two American Air Force bases as well as the establishment of a Royal Air Force training school gave a much-needed boost to the economy.

The Takeoff of Tourism

Eventually, the development dreams of Christie and Oakes came true. North Americans were looking for exotic get-

The Duke of Windsor: A Wartime Visitor

From 1940 to 1945, Edward VIII, Britain's duke of Windsor served as governor of the Bahamas. He had abdicated, or given up, the throne of England, to marry Mrs. Wallis Warfield Simpson, a divorced American.

With war raging in Europe, the duke was sent to the Bahamas for his own protection. It was thought he might be kidnapped by the Nazis, who were battling Great Britain, Canada, the United States, and their Allies.

At first, the Bahamians thought the duke was stiff and unlikable. But he worked hard to improve the economic lot of the people and brought new business to the islands. During a major fire in downtown Nassau in 1942, the duke was one of hundreds of volunteers battling the blaze. After the war, the duke and his wife lived in exile in France.

aways. The Bahamas' warm waters, blue skies, and friendly people attracted thousands of snowbound vacationers from Canada and the United States. Tourism took off and remains an economic mainstay of the country today. Other changes were coming.

In the 1950s, a development board was organized to tackle the Bahamas' recurring economic problems. Business leaders such as Stafford Sands encouraged the building of hotels and tourist attractions and the Bahamas became a haven for international companies. (If businesses had offices in the Bahamas, they did not have to pay any corporate taxes.)

Dr. Doris Johnson: A Suffragette Leader

In 1961, women were finally given the right to vote in the Bahamas. One leader of the country's suffragette movement was Dr. Doris Johnson, who eventually became president of the Bahamian senate.

Although this rule brought money into the country, it didn't do much for ordinary people. Workers went on strike, demanding higher wages and better working conditions.

The United Bahamian Party

For years, wealthy white business owners had run the Bahamas. These men were nicknamed the Bay Street Boys. To protect their financial interests, they formed the United Bahamian Party. They were opposed by the Progressive Liberal Party, a group of black and mixed-race voters. In the late 1950s and early 1960s, the country's black majority demanded a voice in the running of their country.

Sir Roland T. Symonette became premier of the Bahamas in 1964.

There were spirited arguments in the parliament between both parties, especially after a more liberal constitution was drawn up in England in 1964. Sir Roland T. Symonette became the first premier of the Bahamas under the new constitution. He was a successful businessman, chosen to head the country by the United Bahamian Party. Under his administration, Freeport was developed as a business and tourist center. Sir Stafford Sands was named the first minister of finance.

The Progressive Liberals

In the elections of 1967, the Progressive Liberals finally won control of the Assembly. This chain of events transferred control to the new order. It was accomplished peacefully and within the law. But it was still not certain whether the Bahamians wanted full independence from Great Britain.

Through the early 1970s, discussion raged. People argued the point on street corners, in schools, at work, on fishing boats, and in parks. Should we become independent? Or should we not?

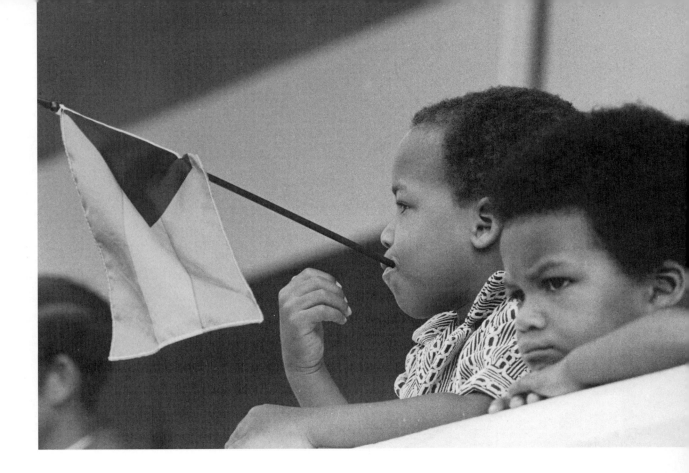

The ties with Great Britain were very strong. The islands' history, language and legal system were English. Many English people had retired to the Bahamas or worked there. However, in the 1972 elections, the Progressive Liberal Party won another general election, defeating several small parties that supported close ties with Great Britain. More talk, compromise, and discussion followed.

It was finally agreed that the Bahamas would strike out on its own. After 250 years as a British colony, the Bahamas became an independent nation on July 10, 1973. The British flag was lowered at midnight over Nassau's Fort Charlotte and the new Bahamian flag raised in its place.

On July 10, 1973, the Bahamas became independent, and citizens waved the new Bahamian flag at the celebrations.

A Land for the People

When independence was achieved in 1973, the Commonwealth of the Bahamas needed a constitution. The new constitution proclaimed the Bahamas as a sovereign democratic state. It set forth requirements for citizenship and guaranteed fundamental human rights such as freedom of conscience, expression, and assembly. The constitution also protected the privacy of the home and prohibited the government from taking someone's property without compensation.

DORIS ADDERLEY

WILLIAM ADDERLEY

JEFFERY BIRCH

PAUL COAKLEY

PETER DOUGLAS

CHARLES GAY

LEROY HANNA

Queen Elizabeth made her first visit to the Bahamas in 1966.

THE BAHAMAS IS PROUD TO BE an independent nation. Its system of government is called a parliamentary democracy, one that holds regular elections for its leaders.

Along with its fierce independence, however, the new nation retains its ties with the British Commonwealth. The Commonwealth is made up of a group of countries that were once ruled by Great Britain. The British monarch remains the head of state for many countries in the Commonwealth, but this is primarily a ceremonial position.

The Royal Influence

The current monarch is Elizabeth II. She became queen in 1952 and has visited the Bahamas for state functions several times during her reign. The local people always turn out for the parades and festivities that mark her visit. A national holiday was declared in 1966 when she arrived for the first time aboard the royal yacht HMS *Britannia*. Many other members of the royal family have visited the islands over the years.

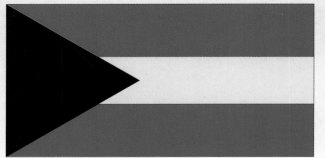

A New National Flag

With independence, a new national flag was adopted. The Bahamian flag now has a black triangle symbolizing the vigor and force of the nation and its inhabitants. A gold bar symbolizing the island's sunny shores cuts across the middle of the flag. Blue bars on the top and bottom represent the waters surrounding the islands.

There are numerous reminders of the British royal presence in the Bahamas. They include the Queen's Staircase, the sixty-five steps leading to Fort Fincastle in Nassau, and the Princess Margaret Hospital, named after that royal visitor in 1955.

The Bahamas National Anthem

"March On Bahamaland"

Lift up your head to the rising sun, Bahamaland;
March on to glory, your bright banners waving high.
See how the world marks the manner of your bearing!
Pledge to excel through love and unity.
Pressing onward, march together to a common
    loftier goal;
Steady sunward, though the weather hide the wide and
    treach'rous shoal.
Lift up your head to the rising sun, Bahamaland;
'Til the road you've trod
Lead unto your God.
March on, Bahamaland.

By Thomas Gibson

The Executive Branch

Queen Elizabeth II appoints a governor general who acts on her behalf as head of state. The first Bahamian-born governor general was Sir Milo B. Butler. He took office in 1973. In 1996, the governor general was Orille Turnquest.

The head of the government is the prime minister. The prime minister is the leader of the majority political party and the nine-member cabinet. The cabinet ministers are responsible for tourism, education, social welfare, security, and related official duties.

Since 1992, the Free National Movement, headed by Prime Minister Hubert A. Ingraham, has governed the Bahamas. Under Ingraham's leadership, the Free National Movement controls thirty-two seats in the Assembly, while the Progressive Liberals, the official opposition, control seventeen seats.

Hubert A. Ingraham, shown campaigning with his wife, became prime minister of the Bahamas in 1992.

A Two-House Parliament

There is a two-house parliament, which consists of a Senate and a House of Assembly. The Senate has sixteen members appointed by the governor general on the advice of the prime minister. Nine members are suggested by the prime minister. Four others are chosen on the advice of the leader of the opposition party. The three remaining members are suggested to the governor general by the prime minister, after talking with the leader of the opposition.

The House of Assembly must have at least forty-nine members, which are elected

Lynden Pindling: The First Prime Minister

The country's first prime minister after independence was the energetic, outspoken Lynden Pindling. He was one of the first members of the Progressive Liberal Party, formed in 1953 to represent the black islanders who made up 85 percent of the Bahamian people. In the final days of colonial rule, Pindling said the voting districts favored the ruling party and did not represent the people. Pindling and his political allies did all sort of things to protest. He once threw the speaker's mace out the window of the parliament, breaking it on the stones outside. The speaker's mace is an emblem of authority used by the parliament's presiding officer.

Pindling, a charismatic leader, attracted large crowds whenever he spoke. He knew the concerns of the Bahamian people and worked hard to help them.

by the people. This number may be increased on the recommendation of the Constituencies Commission, which is charged with reviewing electoral boundaries at least every five years. The current membership was increased to forty-nine in March 1987.

The Courts

The third branch of government is an independent judiciary that includes a Supreme Court and a Court of Appeal. The governor general appoints the chief justice of the Supreme Court on the advice of both the prime minister and the opposition leader. The other justices are also appointed by the governor general. Candidates are recommended by a judicial commission.

The Bahamas judicial system is based on British Common Law, though there is a large volume of Bahamian Statute Law. The highest tribunal in the country is the Court of Appeal. These three judges are leading jurists of the United Kingdom or Commonwealth West Indian nations with no political or business ties to the Bahamas.

Magistrates' courts deal with less serious criminal matters, such as shoplifting and civil matters involving amounts up to $286. A Bahamian citizen can appeal a magistrate's decision to the Supreme Court. An appeal of a Supreme Court decision is directed to the Bahamas Judicial Committee of Her Majesty's Privy Council in England.

Members of the Supreme Court of the Bahamas in traditional dress

The Bahamian constitution can be amended by the parliament, but amendments must also be approved by a referendum—a vote by the people.

Nassau: The Seat of Government

Nassau is the seat of government and, for many people, Nassau *is* the Bahamas. From a cluster of huts built on a hillside overlooking the sea, it has grown to become a major urban area.

When the city was founded in 1670, it was called Charles Town. The city was renamed in 1695 in honor of the Prince of Orange-Nassau who became William III of England. Nassau soon became the center of commerce for the islands due to its protected harbor.

**Nassau:
Did You Know This?**

Population: 171,540

Average January Temperature:
71°F (22°C)

Average July Temperature:
81°F (27°C)

Year Founded: 1670
(as Charles Town)

First Governor: William Sayle

Forts: Fort Nassau (built in 1697), Fort Fincastle (1793), Fort Charlotte (1789)

Major Industry: Tourism

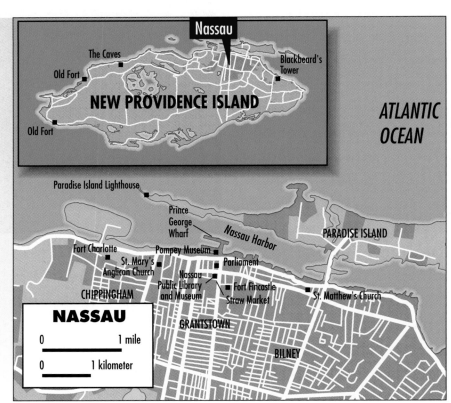

A statue of Queen Victoria
stands in Nassau's
Parliament Square.

Parliament Square is where all the political action takes place. Nearby is a statue of the young Queen Victoria. The square's towering palm trees, lush green grass and riot of vivid blossoms from countless flowers create a peaceful garden in the heart of the city.

Both the House of Assembly and the Senate conduct business in neighboring pink buildings on the square. The city's municipal courts stand along one side of the square. Trials and hearings there are open to the public and provide an interesting look at the British-based legal system.

Behind the House of Assembly is the Supreme Court. You always know when court is in session because the justices walk

The Changing of the Guard

The Changing of the Guard is a time-honored Nassau tradition. The Royal Bahamas Police Force Band cuts a fancy figure with its white pith helmets and starched jackets. The band is well known outside the country. It was a hit at the New York World's Fair in 1964 and 1965 and opened the Olympic Games in Mexico in 1968. The marching unit also won first-place victories in 1978 and 1980 at the National Police Parade competitions held yearly in Rhode Island.

in with their flowing black robes and formal wigs. The traditional clothing is another reminder of the island's British heritage.

On the Bay Street side of the square is the Churchill Building, named after British prime minister Winston Churchill, who led his nation to victory in World War II. The building houses the prime minister's office, ministry of finance, and department of public personnel.

Foreign Policy

The Bahamas is an internationally minded country. Its citizens feel that it is important to help other people.

Bahamians are still proud of the economic summit meeting in Nassau in 1962 attended by U.S. president John F. Kennedy, British prime minister Harold Macmillan, and Canadian prime minister John Diefenbaker. The three leaders planted trees at the intersection of Blake Road and West Bay Street to commemorate the occasion.

The Bahamas' foreign policy is much like those of neighboring democratic nations. For example, it supported the UN Security Council resolution to remove Haiti's military rulers in the early 1990s. The Bahamas also joined the international chorus of voices protesting a coup by the Haitian army that drove out that country's democratically elected government. The Bahamas immediately contributed military personnel to the multinational force that restored the legitimate Haitian political leaders in October 1994.

In addition to the United Nations, the country belongs to the International Civil Aviation Organization, International Criminal Police Organization, the World Bank, and the World Health Organization. It is active in regional affairs and takes the lead in numerous financial, social, and business activities. The Bahamas is also a member of the Caribbean Development Bank, the Caribbean Common Market (CARI-COM), and the Organization of American States.

British prime minister Harold Macmillan (left) and U.S. president John F. Kennedy came to the Bahamas for an economic summit in 1962.

Cooperation with the United States

Since they are geographically so close, the United States and the Bahamas work closely in many areas. They cooperate in law enforcement, marine research, agricultural issues, aviation, meteorology, and maritime safety.

Like the Civil War blockade runners and the Prohibition rumrunners, dope dealers now try to smuggle drugs through the Bahamas to the United States and Canada. Close links between police authorities in each country help slow the traffic.

CHAPTER SIX

Bahamas Business: Boom and Bust

The Bahamian economy used to be a roller-coaster affair. It was either boom or bust. Remember the era of the pirates and their captured treasure? And then came the Confederate blockade runners with their contraband cotton, and the illegal rum of Prohibition era gangsters.

72

S HIPWRECKING, THE SPONGE INDUSTRY, AND PINEAPPLE plantations all had their day. When it was over, sometimes for better and sometimes for worse, the Bahamas often faced an economic slump. Many people lost their jobs and had to leave the islands to find work.

Today, the Bahamian government is doing all it can to correct this economic condition. It is working hard to make the Bahamas more self-sufficient—to diversify its industry and spread out its sources of income.

No Taxes!

The Bahamas does not impose income tax on the people. It raises money by taxing goods shipped into the country. Since the Bahamas does not have a large manufacturing or agricultural base, a great many items are imported, including golf carts, construction machinery, food, and printing paper.

Tourism Industry

Tourism remains the Bahamas' most important industry. Approximately 3.6 million tourists arrive each year to sunbathe, swim, gamble, fish, and explore the reefs. Tourism accounts for more than 85 percent of government revenues and employs almost 66 percent of the labor force. From cab drivers to hotel managers, the people of the Bahamas make sure that visitors are treated well. If people have a good time, they are sure to come back.

However, the tourism picture has not always been rosy. In the late 1980s and early 1990s, there was a drop in the num-

Tourism employs many Bahamians, including this cab driver.

ber of visitors. The U.S. economy was in trouble and there was competition from expanding tourism destinations in nearby countries. Other vacation destinations lured away some visitors. The Bahamians worked hard to respond. Older resorts were renovated and new hotels and guest houses sprang up in Exuma, Abaco, and Eleuthera.

The oldest commercial airline in the world is the Bahamas-based Pan Am Seaplanes, formerly known as Chalk Airlines. Arthur Burns Chalk first started flying passengers from Florida to the islands in 1919, just as Prohibition was starting up in the United States. No one mentioned the fact that much of his cargo was bootleg liquor and that his passengers were gangsters sent to protect the loads. Today, the company's seaplanes visit almost every Bahamian island, ferrying kids, grandmas, and business executives.

Sailing Past and Present

In the days of wooden sailing ships, it was not so easy to get to the Bahamas. Tricky winds and hidden reefs made it a difficult and dangerous voyage. And it still takes about twelve hours to sail from Florida to Bimini—the closest points between the islands and North America. It takes several days to sail from Nassau to Long Island, New York. Travelers have always looked for a safer, faster way to get to the sunny islands.

One answer was steamships. But the first steamer to visit Nassau burned to the waterline just after it docked on May 20, 1851. That accident did not discourage Bahamian business leaders, however. They still saw a great future in luring vacationers out of the frosty winters of the United States and Canada.

In 1859, the year the first Bahamian postage stamp was issued, Samuel Cunard agreed to carry mail and passengers

from New York City to Nassau. Cunard's liners already sailed
the seas between the United States and ports around the
world. So the Bahamians were eager to have these sleek vessels dock in their country. In November, Cunard's SS *Corsica*
arrived amid cheers, fireworks, and brass bands. The ship was
the first of many to stop at Nassau on their way to Cuba.

To serve the passengers, the Royal Victoria Hotel was
built with a government loan and the Bahamas' tourist business was officially born. The hotel was completed just in time
to cash in on the American Civil War and accommodate
hordes of businessmen who came to the Bahamas hoping to
make a fast dollar.

Today, dozens of huge ocean liners bring thousands of tourists to the islands every year. Five piers in Nassau accommodate cruise ships sailing under the flags of several nations.

Passengers flock down the gangplanks from the ships to the end of Prince George Wharf, where a tourist information booth provides assistance. Carriages with lacy fringe tops wait at dockside, ready to take the tourists for a ride around Nassau. Limousines and cabs offer tours of the city's historic sights, beaches, and restaurants. Shuttle boats take gambling fans directly from their ocean liner to the Paradise Island casinos.

A vendor in Nassau's famous Straw Market

Nassau's Straw Market on bustling Market Street is also a popular tourist stop. Shopkeepers advertise their crafts. Girls weave braids and beads into visitors' hair. Children run errands through the crowds.

The cruise ships spend only a day or two in Nassau or Freeport, so their visits are a mixed blessing. Short stays generate less income than longer holidays. Consequently, the government is eager to increase the number of visitors and spread the economic wealth.

Nassau's Royal Bank of Canada is the oldest bank in the Bahamas.

Money was set aside in 1996 to improve harbor facilities on islands other than New Providence. The Bahamas Tourism Bureau also expanded its marketing efforts in Canada and the United States.

A Tax Haven

Financial services are the second most important contributor to the Bahamian economy. The country is a tax haven for corporations and an offshore banking center.

The Bahamas government has long taken an active role in attracting businesses. In 1990, it passed an International

Money Facts

Although Bahamian money looks quite different from U.S. currency, it has the same value. Bahamian bills are printed in bright colors and depict shells, birds, sailboats, fish, and flowers. A portrait of Queen Elizabeth II is on the front of all the bills, which come in denominations of 1, 3, 5, 10, 20, 50, and 100 dollars.

Some coins have unusual shapes, such as the square 15-cent piece with rounded corners. Coins have the following images: 1 cent (starfish); 5 cent (pineapple); 10 cent (bonefish); 15 cent (hibiscus); 25 cent (sailboat); and 50 cent (blue marlin).

Business Companies Act that outlines the financial support and incentives it can give to investors. Targeted next were financial companies and banks. Currently, more than 400 banks and trust companies are located in the Bahamas. About 80 percent are owned by the Royal Bank of Canada and other Canadian financial institutions.

A Duty-Free Zone

A small stream on Grand Bahamas Island became famous in 1955 when it lent its name to an important piece of Bahamian legislation. The Hawksbill Creek Agreement set up a duty-free zone in Freeport, which helped the town become the Bahamas' second-largest city.

Developing Freeport-Lucaya

In the 1950s, Wallace Groves, an American lumberman, suggested turning Freeport into a business center. Groves worked out a development plan with the country's minister of finance, Sir Stafford Sands. Groves was given permission to lease 50,000 acres (20,000 ha) of land from the government and did not have to pay taxes on imports. In exchange, he promised to build a harbor and encourage industry to locate nearby. With these agreements signed, the construction began.

The first successful operation in Freeport was a storage facility for oil. Eventually an oil refinery was built to make oil products and other industries soon followed.

In 1960, Groves decided to add tourism to his Freeport development package. He bought more land and started building casino hotels (bottom), backed by Canadian financier Louis Chesler. They founded a town called Lucaya. Its wide streets, shopping bazaars, and widely spaced homes are very different from the rest of the Bahamas. Today, Freeport looks like a typical suburban community in the United States.

What the Bahamas Grows, Makes, and Mines*	
Agriculture and Fishing	
Crayfish	57.7
Sponges, groupers, and conches	48
Potatoes	23
Manufacturing	
Pharmaceuticals and other chemical products	54.7
Rum	11
Mining	
Salt	15
Aragonite	3.3

*in millions of Bahamian dollars

Today, many businesses set up shop there so that they can store or assemble products in the duty-free zone. They pay no taxes until they ship their goods. This policy makes it profitable to do business in the Bahamas.

An industrial park was then built near the duty-free zone to encourage manufacturing by overseas companies. Every day, business executives arrive by plane at the nearby international airport. Trucks on the Queens Highway haul goods to the harbor. In 1993, the parliament extended the Freeport tax privileges through the year 2054 to ensure that international companies will continue to make profits in the Bahamas.

Arthur Russell, a local boat-builder, manufactures wooden sailboats by hand, in the same way his father and grandfather did.

Industry

Several large manufacturing companies are located elsewhere in the Bahamas. Commonwealth Brewery is based in Nassau and many smaller industries are scattered around the islands.

For more than 150 years, Man-of-War Cay on the Abacos has been the boat-building center for the Bahamas. Boatbuilders often work right on the palm-shaded beach. Blueprints are seldom needed because the builders have years of experience. Valuable woods such as mahogany and teak are used for the decks and railings on fancy sailboats, with Abaco pine used for planking. The fresh scent of timber and the pungent odor of varnish is as much a part of Abaco waterfront life as the scent of flowers.

Nature's vibrant colors provide inspiration to Bahamian industry. The Androsia Company on Andros manufactures hand-painted and naturally dyed cotton-fiber fabrics. After dyeing, the purple, green and yellow batik is hung on clothes-lines to dry in the sun. The cloth is then made into dresses, blouses, scarves, and other clothing sold in upscale shops.

A batik manufacturing company on Andros

Salt Production

Another important Bahamian industry is salt production. Inagua's terrain is perfect for harvesting this valuable commodity. There is little freshwater or rainfall to dilute the salt concentration in the many small lakes on this low-lying island.

Collecting Salt

To collect salt, seawater is pumped into mangrove-lined creeks that flow to depressions in the ground. There it sits until most of the water evaporates. From the air, you can see that salt ponds come in many colors, depending on the type of algae that thrives in the salt water. These tiny plants are important links in the salt production. Their presence increases the water's absorption of heat and speeds up the evaporation process.

The ponds are about 18 inches (45 cm) deep. When the water level drops to a certain point, the remaining liquid is pumped out and the salt crystallizes. The salt is then picked up by bulldozers and cranes and carried in trucks to a storage area for shipping.

Researchers are studying the ponds to see if marine life like crabs and prawns can live there. Several ponds on Long Island are used for this purpose, producing seafood delicacies.

Settlers came to Inagua in the early 1800s to sell salt to passing ships. However, when salt mining began in the United States in the latter part of that century, the Inagua salt industry declined. The United States also put taxes on imported Bahamian salt, which increased its price. Buyers soon turned to the cheaper mainland salt and the bottom dropped out of the Bahamian business.

However, in the 1930s the demand for salt grew and the Bahamian salt industry was revived. The Morton Salt Company eventually bought out several smaller producers.

Farming is still important in the Bahamas, which wants to grow as much of its own food as possible. This allows the Bahamas to save money on importing items.

In the early settlement days, cotton was the main island crop. But an infestation of beetles over several years destroyed the cotton. Subsequently, other crops were tried, including sisal, a fiber used to make ropes. But it was less expensive to produce sisal in India and East Africa so the Bahamian market died out.

Today, modern agricultural techniques such as irrigation and land reclamation are used to ensure healthy vegetable crops. On Great Exuma, marshland has been filled in with rock, sand, and compost. Bat guano (bat dropping) is used as a fertilizer to grow healthy crops of onions. Some farms are small but others employ hundreds of people and ship thousands of bushels of vegetables and avocados from Abaco to Florida.

Agriculture continues to be part of the Bahamian economy. This farmer plows his fields on Andros Island.

Tomatoes are one of the most important vegetables grown on Eleuthera. Vines are planted wherever there is enough soil for their roots and the bright red tomatoes are shipped to canning plants in Nassau. They are sold on the islands, as well as internationally.

At the end of the 1800s, Eleuthera's red soil was also a major pineapple producer. The deliciously sweet product was a favorite in the United States, Canada, and Great Britain. But competition from Hawaii, Cuba, and Puerto Rico drove many planters out of business. Bahamian pineapples were too soft-skinned for easy shipment. In addition, in the early years, Eleuthera did not have a port large enough for freighters to pick up the products. However, with government support, researchers helped develop hardier fruit and better docks were built.

Sugarcane was once thought to be an economic saviour on Abaco. A sugar refinery was built and everyone was excited about the prospects. However, the enterprise was closed after several years of poor harvests. This was the largest agricultural enterprise ever undertaken on the islands by a single company, so its failure was disappointing. Today, the land is used for tree plantations and small-scale vegetable farming.

Exports and Imports

The United States imports about half of all the goods produced and food grown in the Bahamas. Canada is another major buyer, followed by Great Britain and other European countries.

Pineapples for sale on
Harbour Island

The Bahamas imports more than a billion dollars worth of products every year. This includes food, vehicles, auto parts, computers, electronics, and hotel, restaurant, and medical supplies. At least 70 percent of these items come from the United States. The remainder comes from Canada, Great Britain, and Europe.

The People

Eighty-five percent of the 275,000 citizens of the Bahamas today are of African heritage. About two-thirds of the population reside on New Providence Island and in Nassau.

88

T HE FIRST BLACKS IN THE Bahamas were free men, arriving as early as 1656. They were farmers, skilled craft-workers, and tradesmen who came from other islands in the

West Indies and the Caribbean, or from the North American mainland. Like their white neighbors, some blacks became pirates and shipwreckers when economic times were bad.

Not until the 1671 census was there any mention of slaves and "free Negroes" in the islands. While thousands of slaves were eventually imported to work the islands' plantations, free blacks were arriving at the same time. They were taken from wrecked or captured slave ships and set free in the Bahamas. Before the Emancipation Act of 1834 that freed slaves throught the British Empire, some blacks even owned slaves themselves.

Adelaide, a tiny community on the south coast of New Providence Island, was settled in 1831 by Africans rescued from a Portuguese slave ship. The men, women, and children from the captured vessel built homes and started farms. They used techniques they learned in Africa before being captured.

The ruins of a large plantation on Exuma

Free Africans settled elsewhere on New Providence, including Nassau. Creek Village was thriving in the late 1700s and was eventually absorbed into the larger city. The original village was divided into four distinct areas. Free African-born residents lived in Joshua, Congo, and Nango. Burnside Town was settled by those of African descent born in the islands.

Nassau's Gambier Village was settled in 1807 by Africans brought to the Bahamas by the Royal Navy. One resident was Elizah Morris, a former slave. He and other slaves captured a ship off the coast of Abaco in 1840 and made their way to freedom in the Bahamas.

The white population of the Bahamas includes thousands of people who trace their ancestry to the Loyalists. They fled from the new United States and Spanish-controlled Florida after the Revolutionary War. Ruins of their large plantation houses are found everywhere in the Bahamas. One of the few houses still occupied after more than 200 years is The Hermitage on Little Exuma Island.

At first, the Loyalist refugees did not get along well with the white residents already living on the islands. The Loyalists referred to the old-timers as "conchs," after the pink and white mollusk. However, the original white settlers proudly called themselves Old Inhabitants. It took several generations before the two cultures merged under the gentle influence of sun, sand, and sea breezes.

The Loyalists' arrival had another important impact on the Bahamas. They brought so many slaves with them that the racial balance of the islands shifted from about half white and half black to primarily black.

Today, white Bahamians are scattered throughout the islands. Some settlements have the quaint "saltbox" style of square buildings found in New England. Gingerbread trim and brightly painted window shutters are found on homes in Abaco's settlement of New Plymouth, while Duncan Town on Ragged Island looks like an Irish country village. This is not surprising because it was settled by sailors of Irish ancestry.

Both black and white families today carry the names of Loyalist ancestors. For instance, most of the black residents of Long Island in the central Bahamas are named Rolle. They took their name from Lord John Rolle, a Loyalist governor. When he died, Rolle left all his land to his freed slaves and their descendants forever.

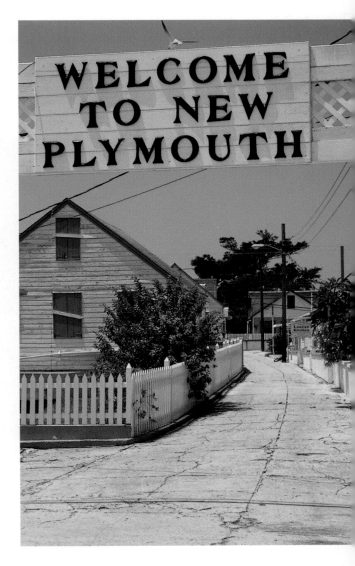

New Plymouth's welcome sign and colorfully painted houses

Friendliness makes everyone feel part of the community. Storytelling is also popular. Bahamian grandparents pass down tales to their grandchildren. Long before television and radio, the past was preserved in this way.

People walk along the sides of roads carrying items on their heads. Black poet Eloise Greenfield wrote a story called "Tradition" that tells you how to carry pumpkins, pineapples, and even chickens on your head, just as people do in Africa.

Much of Bahamian history is passed down from old to young. This portrait shows three generations.

"We carry more than the things you see. We also carry history," she wrote.

The myths of the Bahamas have always been an important part of life on the islands. Making up stories is a time-honored tradition and the stories serve many purposes. They make people feel better about themselves, teach good morals, and keep history alive. These traditions remained strongest on islands where free blacks lived far from the influence of slaveholders.

Since the Emancipation Act

Even after the Emancipation Act of 1834 outlawed slavery, there were social levels on the islands. It was often difficult to move up in this rigid system. This system was based on a racist philosophy that says some people are better than others because of their color. Unfortunately, this idea prevented many Bahamians from reaching their full potential in education and jobs. Although they were in the majority, black Bahamians were always at the bottom of the social ladder, and they were usually poor.

In the center of this system were lower-income whites, the descendants of the Loyalists and the Old Inhabitants. These whites were called "colonials" and considered second-class citizens by those at the top of the social system. But, fearful of losing what little security they had, even the colonials looked down on black Bahamians.

The British colonial administration controlled the island in all aspects. Their candidates ran the Assembly. They owned the major companies. They had the biggest houses and their children went to the best private schools in England, Canada, or the United States.

Generally, the relationship between all parts of Bahamian society was cordial through the years. The Bahamas had none of the rebellions or race riots seen in some other countries during this era. Still, problems lay under this apparently smooth surface. People of the "wrong" color were often not socially welcome in some other Bahamian homes. It was also difficult to find good jobs if an applicant was of the "wrong" color.

However, with the example of the powerful, energetic black leaders of the independence movement, this negative feeling about skin color gradually changed. The progressive public servants and civil rights activists of the 1960s showed their fellow citizens that it was important to be proud of who they were. Race should not make any difference, they said. Today, every shade of citizen is increasingly proud of their past.

Opposite: **The Bahamas has citizens of many different heritages.**

Map of the population

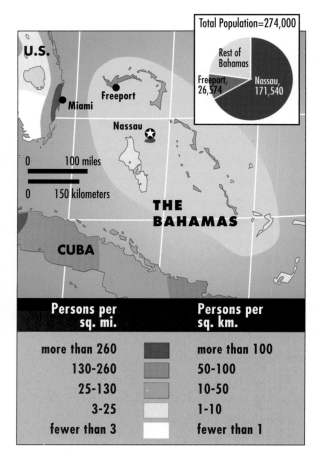

Total Population=274,000

Rest of Bahamas

Freeport, 26,574

Nassau, 171,540

Persons per sq. mi.		Persons per sq. km.
more than 260		more than 100
130-260		50-100
25-130		10-50
3-25		1-10
fewer than 3		fewer than 1

Different Heritages

Although 99 percent of Bahamian citizens are of English heritage and either black or white, there are citizens of many different heritages in the Bahamas.

Chinese were living in the Bahamas as far back as the 1800s. Several thousand Chinese, mostly from Hong Kong, now live in the Bahamas. They feared the Chinese Communist takeover of their city in 1997, after more than one hundred years of British rule. Greeks originally came to the Bahamas to help develop the sponge industry at the turn of the century. Syrians, Jews, and other groups also settled in the Bahamas to live and raise families.

Many Haitians live in the Bahamas. A large percentage are illegal immigrants who fled long years of political repression and found new job opportunities in Nassau. Many Haitians work in Nassau's Straw Market or as laborers on farms. A settlement of Haitians farm on Russell Island, near Spanish Wells on Eleuthera, as well as on some of the other smaller cays.

The Haitians still speak Creole French, a dialect that sounds something like the Cajun French spoken in Louisiana or the Quebec French spoken in Canada.

When Bahamians speak English, it often sounds as if they are singing rather than speaking their words. Over the centuries, the people have picked up words from many other cultures. Irish and Scottish terms liberally spice their conversation, along with African dialects and words handed down from the original settlers.

The language of the Bahamas is colorful, with many expressions pulled from daily life.

Language researchers indicate that the Bahamian sentence structure is similar to that of the rural South in the United

States. In the 1700s, white ancestors of these Southerners moved away from the east coast and settled in Kentucky, Tennessee, Georgia, and Alabama. At this time, British Loyalists fled to the Bahamas. Consequently, the inflections and manner of speaking are somewhat similar. In fact, it is basically considered West Indian English.

Going back even further into history, some common words date to the original Indians of the islands. "Hammock," "cay," "hurricane," "cannibal," and "buccaneer" have found their way into contemporary language.

There are many colorful local speech patterns. For example, if you talk with somebody from "Briland," you know they are from Harbour Island on Eleuthera. Fast-talking residents tend to swallow the name of their town. They drop the "h" in "harbor" and condense two words into one phrase. Thus you hear, "Welcome to Briland," instead of "Welcome to Harbour Island." It is the same with Flamingo Cay in the Exumas. Folks who live there simply say, "Fillimingo" and skip the word "cay."

Bahamian speech is vibrant and alive, full of interesting phrases. "Scrub and scrap" bands are popular in the Abacos. These musicians use ordinary household items for their instruments, which range from washboards to empty cans. The everpresent sea always influences what islanders discuss. Sailors who know the danger of reefs and low tides agree that "a harbor is only a harbor when you can get in and out of it. Otherwise, it's hardly better than a hole in the ground." Or, when the sea is in a "rage," or storming, it is best to stay in port.

The Spiritual Side of Life

Religion is an integral part of Bahamian life. Sunday mornings are filled with song, prayer, and socializing as families flock to the islands' many churches. The church is usually the center of neighborhood life. Weddings, funerals, baptisms, bible studies, picnics, and revival meetings are get-togethers for friends and relatives.

THIRTY-FIVE PERCENT OF THE ENTIRE community is Baptist, making it the predominant church in the Bahamas. Other main denominations include Anglican (Episcopalian) and Roman Catholic. A smattering of other faiths from Islam to Buddhism to Greek Orthodox are also represented on the islands.

After church in the Exumas

Church Services

Religious services in the Bahamas are similar to those in the United States and Canada. A minister or priest usually discusses a Bible passage and communion is often offered to the congregation. There are hymns and gospel songs with lots of handclapping in time with the music. Rhyming spirituals are special to the Bahamas with a lot of "amens" tossed out in response to a verse. These songs were originally brought to the islands by slaves who came from the United States. The spirituals may have religious themes or work-related verses. Some even have a lively calypso beat.

Historic church buildings include the original St. Mary's Anglican Church in Nassau. The building was destroyed in the Great Hurricane of 1866 and rebuilt two years later. It still serves a congregation.

One Bahamian priest, Father Jerome, built churches throughout the islands, including two famous structures at opposite ends of Clarence Town, Long Island. Demonstrating his willingness to help any faith, Father Jerome built St. Paul's Anglican Church on a western hill overlooking the settlement and St. Peter's Catholic Church on an eastern hill.

Religions of the Bahamas

Baptist	35%
Anglican	20%
Roman Catholic	19%
Other*	16%

*Assembly of God, Church of Christ, Church of God, Christian Science, Greek Orthodox, Lutheran, Free Evangelical, Methodist, Presbyterian, Jehovah's Witness, Islam, Baha'i, and Buddhist.

St. Mary's Anglican Church in Nassau

Father Jerome

Father Jerome (1876–1956) was an Anglican who converted to the Roman Catholic faith. His name was originally John Hawes. He traveled all over the world before settling in the Bahamas.

Father Jerome spent his last years on Cat Island where, on Mount Alvernia, he built a small chapel (top) and living quarters with rooms no bigger than closets. He also constructed steps up the mountainside by hand with the Stations of the Cross along the way. These "stations" follow the path of Christ to his crucifixion. Local residents keep the little churchyard clear of weeds and a candle is always kept burning in his memory. Over his grave on the mountain is a sign reading, "Blessed are the dead who died to the Lord."

Oldest Church

Nassau's St. Matthew's Church is the oldest surviving church building in the Bahamas. Opened for service in 1802, the church has a distinctive tower and steeple. The building also has an original stained-glass window dedicated to a bishop of the time. The churchyard contains many old tombs, including that of the editor of the first newspaper to be published in Nassau, the *Bahama Gazette*.

Even with all the established religions in the Bahamas, some Bahamians believe in the supernatural—things that go bump in the night. The origins of Bahamian folk spirits are unclear. Perhaps they came as stories from Africa.

For example, chickcharneys are thought to live deep in the forests of pine and mahogany on Andros Island. These red-eyed, three-fingered, three-toed elves cause plenty of mischief if a passerby surprises them. For better or worse, glass, plastic, and clay chickcharneys line the shelves of souvenir shops in Nassau. They are similar to leprechauns in Ireland or trolls in Scandinavia.

Around Easter time, "spirit creatures" dressed in white or black roam the countryside at night to bedevil humans. Never mind, you can chase these witch-babies away by hitting at them with a branch.

And some say that unearthly voices of long-dead church choirs can be heard on moonlit nights near

Lucayan Beliefs

The long-ago Lucayans believed in two supreme gods, one male and one female. They believed that man had a soul, and upon death, he would go to Coyaba, a place where there was no bad weather, sickness, or unhappiness. Coyaba was a heaven where the Lucayans believed they would find an eternity of feasting and dancing. They also believed in *zemes*, spirits that can bring either good fortune or misfortune.

Warderick Wells, on the south side of Great Exuma Island. However, others say the sound is only that of sea and wind.

On the south shore of San Salvador Island are a cluster of palm trees called the Devil Trees. Many years ago, these trees were hexed to prevent anyone from stealing their coconuts. All sorts of terrible things are supposed to happen to a thief because of the hex.

Obeah

Wherever African slaves settled, some of their beliefs, healing techniques, and superstitions came with them. These were combined with European superstition and religion to form a belief called Obeah, which is practiced throughout the Caribbean and Brazil. Obeah is thought to bring about good or evil, cure the sick, and cause the poor to become rich—or the rich to become poor.

Many Obeah practioners learned their skills from an older person but some claim to have had their gifts since birth. Others get their powers as adults, by going into a trance. When they wake up, they say they have learned the secrets of Obeah.

The Spiritual Side of Life **103**

Obeah masters can "fix," or cast a spell, on someone. It is believed that whatever the spell is supposed to do, it will do. The right words can make someone fall in love or help win a ballgame or make a business succeed.

If you are fixed by an Obeah master, you can only be "cleared," or cured, by another Obeah practitioner. But if you are cursed, only the person who put the curse on you can take it away.

A practicer of voodoo

Voodoo

The Haitians who came to the Bahamas brought the practice of voodoo with them. Voodoo is a mixture of African traditions and Christian religion. The word *voodoo* comes from *vodu*, which originated in Dahomey, an ancient kingdom that was once the center of the slave trade on the West African coast.

Some Bahamians feel that voodoo is more powerful than Obeah. It is said that Bahamians who die are taken to Haiti and become "zombies," or the living dead. A joke during Bahamian elections says that some politicians go to Haiti and bring these zombies back to vote!

This popular bush-medicine expert holds a papaya, one of her favorite remedies.

Bush Medicine

Bush medicine, the use of bushes, barks, and herbs for healing, goes far back in history. Islanders used these natural materials for medicine because there were few doctors available. Travel from island to island was also time-consuming and difficult for medical personnel. Today, medical experts agree that certain plants have healing powers.

The Creative
Way of Life

Creativity seems to blossom in the sunny Bahamas. Locals and visitors alike quickly tune in to the rhythms of the island's cultural life. The colors of nature draw artists. The tranquility attracts writers. Athletes can train all year round, and outdoor lovers, such as sailors, golfers, and fishing fans, enjoy the weather every day.

Readers take advantage of the Nassau Public Library.

READING IS IMPORTANT ON THESE islands. The country's literacy rate is almost 100 percent—that's higher than in the United States. There are six public libraries in the nation as well as a library in every school.

The Nassau Public Library and Museum, built in the 1700s, was originally a prison. The historical old building was restored, redecorated, and transformed into a place of learning. It now has more than 70,000 books, and a special area where kids can sprawl around and read.

Literature

The islands are home to several well-known authors. Young readers love the funny *B'ooky and B'rabby* book by Dr. Peter Maynard. Schoolchildren enjoy performing in a play called *Woman Take Two*, written by Telcin Turner Rolle. Rolle also has a collection of stories and poems called *Climbing Clouds*.

Lively verses by James Catalyn, a Bahamian actor-poet, focus on his country's ever-changing society and its increasing pride. He also touches on such serious subjects as the effects of slavery. Patricia Glinton-Meicholas wrote *Talking Bahamian*,

a book that discusses the religions, bush medicine, and other aspects of everyday Bahamian life.

Writing about the Bahamas is nothing new. Since the 1500s, travelers have described the beauty and tranquility of the islands. Bliss Carmen, a noted poet of the 1800s, regularly visited the Bahamas. His *White Nassau* describes the life there in such verses as

> *"Look from your door and tell me now*
> *The color of the sea.*
> *Where can I buy that wondrous dye*
> *And take it home with me?"*

Painting Scene

Many artists have painted the wonderful Bahamian landscape. American artist Winslow Homer was the most famous. He regularly traveled to Nassau, developing an easily identifiable, realistic style in watercolors and oils. His most famous painting is *The Gulf Stream*, completed in 1899.

One of the best-known contemporary Bahamian artists is Amos Ferguson of Exuma. His vibrant colors and strong Bahamian themes leap out from the canvas. Ferguson's paintings have been widely shown at museums in the United States, and an award-winning documentary of his life was presented on U.S. public television.

Ernest Hemingway—Literary Vacationer

Novelist Ernest Hemingway came to Bimini often. He loved the fishing, the sunshine, and the chance to work in peace. On one fishing expedition, he caught a 795-pound (360-kg) mako shark.

Between his fishing trips, Hemingway found time to finish a novel entitled *To Have and Have Not*. He was working on *Islands in the Stream* when he died in 1961. That book describes the excitement of deep-sea fishing off Alice Town, a settlement on North Bimini.

Harbour Island's Eddie Minnis is another talented Bahamian painter. His enchanting landscapes show his keen, observing eye. He is also an architect, a busy songwriter, a recording artist, and a cartoonist.

Historian and author Ruth Wolper is an expert on Christopher Columbus. She relaxes by painting portraits of the famous explorer.

A public mural in Nassau

Artist Amos Ferguson stands with his artwork.

Albert Lowe was a famous artist who lived in New Providence, Abaco. He painted the people of the Loyalist community there as they went about their daily lives. His son Alton, also an artist, runs a museum that displays much of the elder Lowe's work.

Theater

The Dundas Center for the Performing Arts, the only full-time professional theater in the Bahamas, is directed by playwright Winston Saunders, noted author of *You Can Bring a Horse to Water*. The theater presents plays, musicals, and bal-

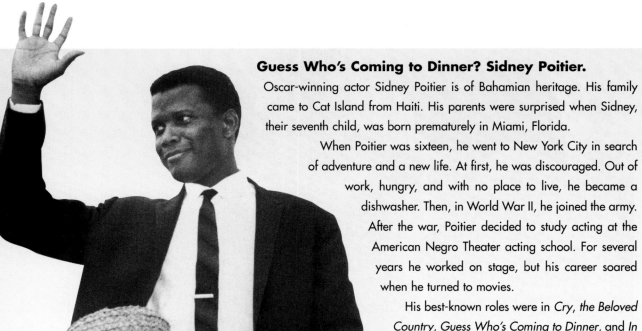

Guess Who's Coming to Dinner? Sidney Poitier.

Oscar-winning actor Sidney Poitier is of Bahamian heritage. His family came to Cat Island from Haiti. His parents were surprised when Sidney, their seventh child, was born prematurely in Miami, Florida.

When Poitier was sixteen, he went to New York City in search of adventure and a new life. At first, he was discouraged. Out of work, hungry, and with no place to live, he became a dishwasher. Then, in World War II, he joined the army. After the war, Poitier decided to study acting at the American Negro Theater acting school. For several years he worked on stage, but his career soared when he turned to movies.

His best-known roles were in *Cry, the Beloved Country*, *Guess Who's Coming to Dinner*, and *In the Heat of the Night*. Poitier won his 1963 Oscar for *Lilies of the Field*.

lets. Bahamian actors such as Greg Lampkin and Vivica Watkins often star in these productions.

Actors from such amateur theater companies as the Bahamas Drama Circle, Nassau Players, and University Players also present excellent shows.

Movies and James Bond

Filmmakers are also drawn to the islands because they don't have to worry about losing a day of shooting due to bad weather.

English author Ian Fleming's vacations in the Bahamas inspired several James Bond spy novels that eventually became movies. Fleming imagined the setting for *Dr. No* (1962) after a visit to hot, dry Inagua. *Thunderball* (1965) was filmed mainly amid the casino glitter of Paradise Island. And *Never Say Never Again* (1983) was photographed at several spots on the islands, including Nassau's Straw Market.

The Bahamas is also a great place for well-known personalities to settle. Actor Sean Connery, who starred in many James Bond movies, enjoyed the Bahamas so much that he became a part-time resident of Lyford Cay. However, tourists hardly ever get a glimpse of this famous guest—the resort is known for ensuring privacy for its famous visitors.

Music

Musical talent is everywhere in the Bahamas, from the rock bands in Out Island nightclubs to chamber orchestras in Nassau. The Bahamas Music Society and Nassau Music Society sponsor

opera and concerts. The Nassau Operatic Society, the Renaissance Singers, the Chamber Singers, and the Lucayan Chorale perform throughout the islands. Other local musicians, like harmonica player Jimmy Bowlegs, perform on street corners for the enjoyment of visitors and locals.

Athletic Success

Along with artists, writers, and actors, the Bahamas has produced many fine athletes. Baseball, basketball, tennis, volleyball, swimming, and track and field are among the more popular sports in high school.

Many Bahamian students go on to college in the United States, where they continue their sports activities. Debbie Ferguson, born in Nassau in 1976, was a four-time All-American sprint champion while a premed student at the University of Georgia.

The Olympics offer opportunities as well. The Bahamian women's track team won the silver medal in the 400-meter relay in the 1996 Summer Olympics in Atlanta, Georgia. Bahamian tennis stars Roger Smith and Mark Knowles also made strong showings at the Olympics in Atlanta.

Basketball

It seems that every vacant lot in the Bahamas has been turned into a basketball court. Kids play constantly, even after spending long hours practicing with their school teams.

Some players have been snared by the pros in the United States. Nassau-born Mychal Thompson was picked by the Portland Trail Blazers in 1978 after finishing college at the University of Minnesota. He then played in Portland for seven years. However, he broke his leg on a visit back home and had to sit out one season. He next played center-forward for the Los Angeles Lakers from 1986 to 1991.

Opposite: **Harmonica player Jimmy Bowlegs performs on street corners.**

Basketball is one of the most popular sports in the Bahamas.

While every Bahamian athlete doesn't make it to the National Basketball Association or the Olympics, sports remain the most popular activity for many young Bahamians. The Bahamas Amateur Athletic Association hosts championships between the islands in volleyball, basketball, baseball, and softball. Many clubs cater to kids and their sports interests.

Fishing

Everyone enjoys fishing in the Bahamas. Hand-line fishing is the easiest and cheapest way to catch your dinner. All you need is a hook, line, and bait. A boat helps, but hand-lining can be done from a rock. The rising tide is the best time for this method of fishing. Look for a large clump of coral reef or a headland jutting into the ocean—that's where the fish like to hide.

A glass-bottomed boat allows you to see the fish lurking below the surface of the water. Bait a hook with conch or crabmeat, toss the weighted line overboard and wait for a "pick," or nibble.

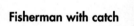

Fisherman with catch

An experienced fisherman can often tell the type of fish by the pick. A slow tug means you've got a large grouper or snapper, while a faster pick is probably a triggerfish or something smaller. Let's hope a hungry barracuda does not gobble up the catch before you can pull it out of the water.

Then there's deep-sea fishing. Imagine hooking a 20-foot- (6-m-) long hammerhead shark that roars out of the ocean at your boat! Yet after a long, tiring tussle, you finally win the match. Back on the dock, the shark is strung up on a scale and photos are taken of the prize.

The best sport comes in battling marlin, sailfish, and swordfish, which can weigh 500 pounds (227 kg) or more. Every fishing guide has a special way of catching fish. But their techniques all boil down to one thing: it's one person fighting one fish.

Water Sports for Tourists

Visitors always enjoy outdoor activities. Naturally, many outdoor sports focus on the ocean. Scuba diving and snorkeling are popular. Photographers use special cameras to take underwater pictures of exotic fish amid the colorful reefs. Other popular water sports include sailing, waterskiing, windsurfing, and parasailing.

Parasailing

Parasailing in the Bahamas is mostly for tourists. A number of Bahamians, however, also parasail.

First, you are taken out to a small raft about 1 mile (1.6 km) offshore. There, you are strapped into a safety jacket and harness attached to a parachute that is laid out carefully behind you. Ropes from the harness are then hooked to the rear of a motorboat.

When the boat gets up speed, you run to the edge of the raft and jump into the air. The boat's momentum is enough to jerk you skyward immediately. If not, you are dragged through the water until the parachute catches the wind. Then you fly to a height of least several hundred feet where you have a fantastic view of the sea and the islands.

The ocean there is so clear that you can see fish swimming far below the surface. When the boat slows, you float down. The goal is to land gently on the launch raft. But if you miss the raft, the motorboat is always close enough for a speedy rescue.

Up and At 'Em

Jimmy Gage wakes up early on the first Saturday of December. Saturday is usually his day to sleep in after a long week at school. But today, he is too excited to sleep late. He wants to start making his Junkanoo costume. Jimmy jumps out of bed and pulls on his jeans and his favorite T-shirt. In the kitchen, his mother is preparing breakfast. She is a great cook and works part-time in the hotel his father manages on Nassau's Cable Beach.

TODAY, JIMMY AND HIS FRIENDS ARE GOING TO THE JUNKANOO Expo on the waterfront. The Expo is a museum packed with colorful creations from past Junkanoo parades.

Jimmy and his friends look around the museum and pick their favorite costumes. He likes a green, blue, red, and orange outfit with a matching hat that stands 2 feet (60 cm) high. His mother is going to help him make his costume. Jimmy wants to have the best costume and he has been saving crepe paper for three months. The weekend before Christmas, he and his buddies will be in the Junior Junkanoo competition. They want to beat the other schools this year and take the trophy back to their school.

Junkanoo

The origins of Junkanoo are lost in history but the word was probably taken from "John Canoe." This might have been the English name of an African chief or a ship's captain who once visited Africa. It might also have evolved from the Yoruba word, *gensinconnu*, meaning "a person wearing a mask." Yorubas were among the thousands of African slaves brought to the Bahamas to work on plantations. The Yoruba wore face coverings and elaborate costumes during ceremonies worship-

ing their ancestors. Perhaps today's celebration comes from that long-ago heritage.

Whatever its origin, Junkanoo is upbeat, loud, and fun. Music is pounded out on goatskin drums, accompanied by whistles, horns, and cowbells. The parades are usually held the day after Christmas. Other Junkanoo celebrations come after New Year's Day. Many Junkanoo clubs prepare for the holiday parades throughout the year. They compete for best costumes, best music, and best floats. Even members of parliament and other government officials join in the fun.

A Junkanoo participant

Jimmy's Afternoon

After coming home from the museum, it's time for lunch and violin practice. Until the ninth grade, all Bahamian students have to take lessons on a musical instrument. Jimmy practices for half an hour, then enjoys a conch salad with his mother. His sister, Ruth, a bank teller in downtown Nassau, is having lunch with friends.

Holidays and Festivals

During slavery days in the Bahamas, everyone looked forward to the four annual holidays—Christmas, Boxing Day, New Year's Day, and Easter. Boxing Day falls the day after Christmas. It is an English holiday on which servants were given Christmas presents in boxes.

After slavery was abolished, people of African descent celebrated Emancipation Day and Fox Hill Day (Fox Hill is an area of Nassau). These holidays were meaningful for the Bahamians because they celebrated the freedom of the people. These festivities included dancing, singing, and feasting but they have faded into the past as the Bahamas became a modern nation.

Goombay is a festival series, similar to Junkanoo (top), held in the summer. Costumed drummers and dancers perform on Wednesday nights along Bay Street in Nassau, mainly to entertain tourists.

After lunch, Jimmy meets his pals at the school playground for some basketball. Then one of the mothers gives them a ride to the beach. As the sun goes down, the boys head home.

Supper

Jimmy's mother often brings home treats from the restaurant. With luck there is some leftover sweet potato stuffed with crabmeat, or smoked turbot and spinach roll wrapped in bacon. Ruth and Jimmy help their mother make supper. Tonight, the family feasts on baked crab, peas, and rice, with coconut and pineapple for desert. They usually have some kind of seafood at their meals because it is always fresh and inexpensive.

Conch salad consists of conch meat, vegetables, and lime or lemon juice.

After supper, Jimmy and his mother plan his Junkanoo costume while his father reads the *Nassau Guardian* and the *Nassau Tribune*. The *Guardian*, first published in 1844, is the morning paper while the *Tribune*, a newspaper that dates back to 1903, is delivered in the evening.

Jimmy's father tunes in to a radio station that plays oldies music. Jimmy prefers a more modern rock music station. He usually watches television later in the evening. The Gages can pick up broadcast signals from Florida, Cuba, and Mexico on their satellite dish.

An extended family watches television at home.

Television

ZNS-13, the only television station on the islands, is managed by the Broadcasting Corporation of the Bahamas. It transmits from New Providence and can be seen for 130 miles (209 km) around Nassau. But the station operates for only six hours a day on weekdays, sixteen hours on Saturday, and twelve hours on Sunday.

The station airs many programs produced in the United States and Great Britain. News is aired nightly, and church programs take up much of the Sunday programing.

A Game of Warri

On most Sundays, he meets his grandfather for a game of *warri*. They arrange their warri boards on tables set up under the palm trees in a nearby park. Warri is an ancient game enjoyed by both adults and children. It is played all over Africa but under different names. In Nigeria, the game is called *ayo*.

Back to School

Jimmy usually enjoys school, although the weather is always so pleasant that it is sometimes hard to sit at his school desk and concentrate. Every weekday, he crawls out of bed and puts on his school uniform—dark pants and a white shirt. Jimmy is glad he doesn't have to worry about what to wear. All the boys

How to Play *Warri*

Two players sit on either side of a long board that has six holes on each side. Four small seeds are placed in each hole. The first player picks up all the seeds in the first hole and moves them clockwise one by one to the next holes until his handful is gone. Then it is the second player's turn to move the seeds from a hole on his side. This goes on, back and forth. Eventually, the seeds begin to pile up in some of the holes.

Each player captures as many seeds from the next hole as possible when it is his or her turn to move. The first player to run out of seeds loses this fast-paced game. With experienced players, a game of warri can be over in a few minutes.

in his school wear the same clothes and the girls wear red and green plaid skirts with white blouses.

Classes start at 9 A.M. Sometimes Jimmy can hardly wait until 3 P.M. when classes are over. In the Bahamas, schooling is compulsory between the ages of five and fourteen.

The government runs 177 of the 220 schools in the Bahamas. The other 43 schools are operated by religious groups such as the Methodists, Catholics, Episcopalians, and Presbyterians. The total enrollment amounts to more than 60,000 students. Every island has its own schools. The larger islands, like New Providence, have several high schools.

All children from ages five to fourteen must attend school.

A high-school physics class

Education is free, but parents are expected to provide some of the textbooks. Jimmy studies science, mathematics, English, as well as arts and crafts, like most students in Canada and United States.

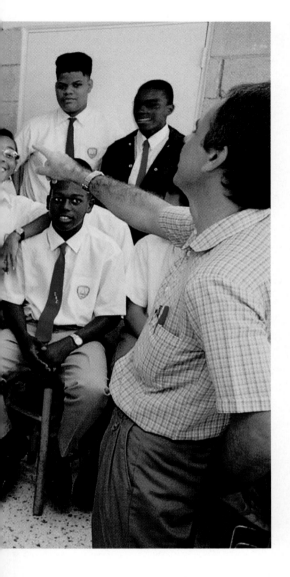

After High School

In high school, students decide whether to take courses that will prepare them for college or vocational classes such as welding, plumbing, drafting, or electronics. Technical high schools on Grand Bahama and New Providence teach mechanics, dressmaking, business and marketing, computer skills, and other subjects. After graduation, the students usually get on-the-job training in an apprentice program.

Jimmy wants to study business at the College of the Bahamas in Nassau, the only four-year college on the islands. Some of his friends will probably go to universities in Britain, the United States, or Canada. Others may go to the University of the West Indies in Jamaica, Barbados, or Trinidad. One of Jimmy's friends wants to become a lawyer. She will go to a large law school at the University of the West Indies in Barbados.

Hosting Visitors

On Monday, when his parents come home from work, Jimmy's dad says the Gages have been asked to host an American family visiting the Bahamas. The Bahamas Tourism Office runs a popular program that arranges for visitors to spend time with Bahamians and learn more about the country.

Jimmy remembers the time his family hosted a family from Toronto. It was fun showing kids from another country around Nassau and New Providence Island. They watched the Changing of the Guard ceremony outside Government House one Saturday and went out to eat after the Royal Bahamas Police Force Band marched past.

Jimmy uses a school computer to e-mail his new friend. They talk mostly about sports stars and movies. The Gages' guests this time will be a family with three sons from Atlanta, Georgia. Jimmy is hoping the boys like to play basketball.

The lighthouse at Nassau

Timeline

History of the Bahamas

		World History
	c. 2500 B.C.	Egyptians build the Pyramids and Sphinx in Giza.
	563 B.C.	Buddha is born in India.
	A.D. 313	The Roman emperor Constantine recognizes Christianity.
The Caribs push the Lucayans out of what is now Venezuela and the Lucayans settle the Inaguas.	600	
	610	The prophet Muhammad begins preaching a new religion called Islam.
	1054	The Eastern (Orthodox) and Western (Roman) Churches break apart.
	1066	William the Conqueror defeats the English in the Battle of Hastings.
	1095	Pope Urban II proclaims the First Crusade.
	1215	King John seals the Magna Carta.
	1300s	The Renaissance begins in Italy.
	1347	The Black Death sweeps through Europe.
	1453	Ottoman Turks capture Constantinople, conquering the Byzantine Empire.
Christopher Columbus lands at San Salvador and claims the islands for Spain.	1492	
A systematic deportation of Lucayans for slave labor in South America begins.	1500	
	1500s	The Reformation leads to the birth of Protestantism.
Ponce de León visits the Bahamas.	1513	
The Eleutherian Adventurers set up a colony in Governor's Bay.	1648	
English colonists settle New Providence.	1656	
A group of wealthy businessmen are given the right to colonize the Bahamas.	1670	

History of the Bahamas

The Spanish sack and raze New Providence.	1684
The pirate Blackbeard makes his headquarters in Fort Nassau.	1705
Woodes Roger becomes the first royal governor and fights against piracy.	1718
The Bahamas surrender to the Spanish.	1782
The Bahamas are officially returned to the British.	1783
English Loyalists flee the new United States of America to settle in the Bahamas.	1783 – 1784
The Emancipation Act outlawing slavery throughout the British Empire is passed.	1834
The Bahamas is used as a base for blockade-running to Southern ports in the American Civil War.	1861 – 1864
One of the worst hurricanes in history strikes the Bahamas.	1866
Rumrunners set up in the Bahamas to ship rum illegally to America during Prohibition.	1920 – 1933
Islands are used as a U.S. military base during World War II.	1940 – 1945
A new Bahamian constitution is drawn up in Britain.	1964
The Progressive Liberal Party wins control of the government.	1967
The Bahamas becomes an independent nation, with Lynden Pindling as prime minister.	1973
Hubert A. Ingraham, the leader of the Free National Movement, is elected prime minister.	1992

World History

1776	The Declaration of Independence is signed.
1789	The French Revolution begins.
1865	The American Civil War ends.
1914	World War I breaks out.
1917	The Bolshevik Revolution brings Communism to Russia.
1929	Worldwide economic depression begins.
1939	World War II begins, following the German invasion of Poland.
1957	The Vietnam War starts.
1989	The Berlin Wall is torn down, as Communism crumbles in Eastern Europe.
1996	Bill Clinton is reelected U.S. president.

Fast Facts

Official name: Commonwealth of the Bahamas

Nassau

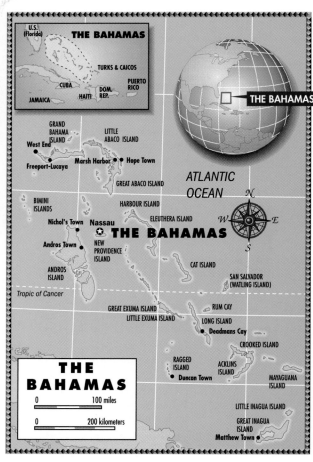

Capital: Nassau

Official language: English

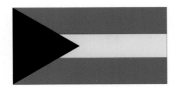

Flag of the Bahamas

Official religion:	None
National anthem:	"March On Bahamaland," by Thomas Gibson
Founding date:	1670, as British protectorate; July 10, 1973, as Commonwealth of the Bahamas
Founder:	William Sayles (as British protectorate), Lynden O. Pindling (as Commonwealth of the Bahamas)
Government:	Constitutional monarchy with two legislative houses
Chief of state:	British monarch
Head of government:	Prime minister
Area:	5,382 square miles (13,939 sq km), with more than 2,000 islands spread over 103,000 square miles (266,770 sq km)
Nearest countries:	United States, Cuba, Haiti, and Dominican Republic
Highest elevation:	Mount Alvernia, 206 feet (63 m)
Lowest elevation:	Sea level

Average temperatures:

in June	*in December*
80°F (27°C)	70°F (21°C)

Average annual rainfall:	44 inches (112 cm)
National population (1995):	274,000

Population of largest cities:

Nassau	171,540
Freeport-Lucaya	26,574

Island populations:

Abaco	10,003
Acklins Island	405
Andros	8,155
Bimini Islands	1,639
Cat Island	1,698
Crooked Island	412
Eleuthera	10,524
Exuma Island	3,556
Grand Bahama	40,898
Harbour Island	1,219
Inagua Islands	985
Long Island	3,400
Mayaguana	312
New Providence	172,196
Ragged Island	89
Rum Cay	53
San Salvador	465
Spanish Wells	1,372

Famous landmarks: The Bahamas is best known for its beaches and underwater views of ocean life. Historic sites include several eighteenth-century forts and churches, Straw Market, the Pompey Museum, and Parliament Square in Nassau. On San Salvador are the New World Museum and monuments commemorating Christopher Columbus and the Lucayan Indians. Hope Town, on the east coast of Great Abaco, is noted for its candy-cane-striped lighthouse overlooking the harbor and the Wyannie Malone Historical Museum.

Industry: In the Bahamas, tourism is the most important industry. Banking is the islands' second most profitable business. Crayfishing, food-processing, pharmaceutical manufacturing, and salt production also contribute to the economy.

Currency: One Bahamian dollar equals one U.S. dollar; both are accepted on the islands.

Weights and measures: Imperial system

Literacy: Virtually 100%

To Find Out More

Nonfiction

▶ Brothers, Don. *West Indies*. New York: Chelsea House, 1989.

▶ Evans, F. C., and R. N. Young, *The Bahamas*. Cambridge: Cambridge University Press, 1976.

▶ Lee, Sally. *Hurricanes*. New York: Franklin Watts, 1993.

▶ McCulla, Patricia E. *Bahamas*. New York: Chelsea House, 1988.

▶ McWilliams, Karen. *Pirates*. New York: Franklin Watts, 1989.

▶ Springer, Eintou P. *The Caribbean*. Morristown, N.J.: Silver Burdett Press, 1987.

Biography

▶ Bergman, Carol. *Sidney Poitier*. New York: Chelsea House, 1988.

▶ Blassingame, Wyatt. *Ponce de Leon*. New York: Chelsea House, 1991.

▶ Meltzer, Milton. *Columbus and the World Around Him*. New York: Franklin Watts, 1990.

Folklore

▶ Edwards, Charles L. *Bahamas Songs and Stories: A Contribution to Folklore.* New York: Gordon Press, 1976.

Reference

▶ Albury, Paul. *The Story of the Bahamas.* New York: St. Martin's Press, 1975.

▶ Craton, Michael. *A History of the Bahamas.* London: Collins, 1962.

Websites

▶ **Bahamas On-Line**
http://thebahamas.com
Provides information about Bahamian history and culture, a calendar of local events, and a hurricane tracker.

▶ **The Bahamas Ministry of Tourism**
http://www.interknowledge.com/bahamas
Provides travel information, maps, and photographs of the islands.

Organizations and Embassies

▶ **Embassy of the Commonwealth of the Bahamas**
2220 Massachusetts Avenue, NW
Washington, DC 20008
(202) 319-2660

▶ **Bahamas Ministry of Tourism**
150 East 52nd Street
New York, NY 10022
(800) 422-4262

Index

Page numbers in *italics* indicate illustrations

Meet the Authors

Gathering information for *The Bahamas* involved several trips to the islands for father and son Martin and Stephen Hintz. On these excursions, they met Bahamians, explored blue holes, ate oodles of conch, watched Junkanoo dancers, and sailed. Steve draped a snake around his neck, went parasailing, watched flamingos, played basketball, and snorkeled over colorful reefs.

During their visit, the authors met families through the Bahamian People-to-People program and talked with cab drivers, tour guides, historians, journalists, chefs, tourism officials, librarians, entertainers, and politicians.

In addition to visiting the Bahamas, the Hintzes scanned the Internet and used the Bahamas Ministry of Tourism's website. The U.S. State Department in Washington, D.C., provided briefing papers on the political and business scene in the Bahamas.

Libraries were another rich resource. Histories of the islands, biographies of explorers and pirates, guidebooks, and journals written by sailors provided all sorts of useful material.

In collecting and organizing material, Martin and Steve were aided by intern Kathleen Daley, who confirmed facts and got more details.

Martin Hintz is a travel writer with more than forty books and hundreds of magazine and newspaper articles to his credit. He has written eleven books in the previous Enchantment of the World series, many of which have won awards.

Steve Hintz has also assisted Martin in researching and writing Birnbaum and Frommer travel guides. The two authors also collaborated on the award-winning *Family Adventure Guide to Wisconsin* (1996, Globe Pequot Publishing).

Steve is a 1996 graduate of the University of Wisconsin-Milwaukee with a degree in sociology and African-American studies. He first visited the Bahamas when he was sixteen.

Photo Credits